DAY BY DAY

Make sure I get International Plan

Mandy (Taiwan)
267-867-6695

Rod (Australia)
415-513-0382

Rachel (Israel)
216-513-1253

Carrie (Australia)
617-849-8456

Margaret NY
    Home 585-465-0530
KS ↗ (Askher)
    323-674-1124 (?.)

Day by Day

DAILY MEDITATIONS
FOR RECOVERING ADDICTS

Hazelden
Publishing

Hazelden
Center City, Minnesota 55012-0176
1-800-328-0094
http://www.hazelden.org

Library of Congress Cataloging-in-Publication Data
Day by day : daily meditations for recovering addicts.
        p.   cm.
    Originally published in 1974.
    Includes index.
ISBN-13: 978-1-56838-234-0 ISBN-10: 1-56838-234-0
    1. Recovering addicts—Prayer-books and
devotions—English. 2. Devotional calendars.
BL625.9.R43D38   1998
616.86'03—dc21   98-14608
                                            CIP

            2015   16 15 14

    Book design by Will H. Powers
    Cover design by David Spohn
Typesetting by Stanton Publication Services, Inc.

Look to this day,
For it is life,
The very life of life.
In its brief course lie all
The realities and verities of existence,
The bliss of growth,
The splendor of action,
The glory of power—

For yesterday is but a dream,
And tomorrow is only a vision,
But today, well lived,
Makes every yesterday a dream
    of happiness
And every tomorrow a vision of hope.

Look well, therefore, to this day.

SANSKRIT PROVERB

Lord, make me an
instrument of Your peace!

Where there is hatred—let me sow love
Where there is injury—pardon
Where there is doubt—faith
Where there is despair—hope
Where there is darkness—light
Where there is sadness—joy

O Divine Master, grant that I
may not so much seek

To be consoled—as to console
To be understood—as to understand
To be loved—as to love
                              for
It is in giving—that we receive
It is in pardoning—that we are pardoned
It is in dying—that we are born to eternal life.

PRAYER OF SAINT FRANCIS

JANUARY 1

Living today

The beginning of the New Year will often bring back sad memories. This has been the big day for hangovers, coming down, remorse, guilt, and shame. But if we stay with our new purpose—staying clean and staying close to our Higher Power—we don't have to fear the New Year. God has forgiven our past mistakes and tomorrow is not yet here. If we do what we know is right today, all else will be taken care of.

It's not always easy to do what is necessary today, but it's *impossible* to change yesterday or to guarantee what tomorrow will bring. Our year will unfold better by living each day as it comes instead of regretting the past or anticipating the future.

Am I learning to live one day at a time?

> I pray for the willingness to deal with today, instead of being obsessed with the past or the future.

> *My plan for living today is*

God help me to stay clean and sober today!

JANUARY 2

Letting go of results

Some of us are familiar with the saying "Plan plans, not results." For those of us with addictive or compulsive personalities this is a very important message. Our heads can spin so much with the results we plan for tomorrow that we forget what we need to do for a good life today.

If we "plan" to have a partner, $5,000 in the bank, and a new home by this time next year, chances are we will blow it. We know from experience that if we take that first fix, pill, or drink we will have nothing at this time next year.

Do I know how to plan well?

> **I pray to do the necessary footwork today and leave the results with my Higher Power.**

The results I will leave to God today are

God help me to stay clean and sober today!

JANUARY 3

Asking how

Many days we are tempted to ask *Why? Why* did this happen to me? *Why* was I singled out? *Why* am I not a different person? But the whys lead only to clever explanations and rationalizations of what we do or what we are. The question for us is not *Why?* but *How?*

We ask how to learn and work our program of recovery; the "how" can give us a deeper understanding of the program. We ask God *How?* and God provides the strength and guidance needed. "How" will lead to everything needed for recovery and personal growth. "Why" is irrelevant.

Am I learning *how* to live?

> Higher Power, teach me how to
> live, love, and learn.

Today I will ask how to

God help me to stay clean and sober today!

Learning new ways

Once we make a connection with our Higher Power, the ongoing problem is to hold on to it. Repeatedly we slip into our old ways of thinking and behaving. If not curtailed, eventually these will lead us back to that first fix, pill, or drink. We need only a word, thought, or familiar situation to get caught up again in an old habit.

We have to discover (and rediscover) that the old way of life has become impossible and the new one essential. We do this—and do it again—by praying, meditating, and working the Twelve Steps of recovery.

Am I living the program?

Higher Power, help me avoid being smug
and complacent in my new life.
Remind me that old ways of living have
become impossible for me.

*The new ways of living
that I will cultivate today are*

God help me to stay clean and sober today!

Being able to be wrong

We had to compete with everyone, sometimes subtly, sometimes less subtly. We always had to be right; to be wrong seemed unbearable. We could never seem to bring ourselves to say simply, "I was wrong." We were afraid of what would happen to us if we did. Our egos were very fragile; we were never as strong as we had led ourselves to believe.

We came to discover, however, that real strength comes from being able to be wrong and from being willing to change our ways of thinking and living.

Can I face being wrong and learn from it?

Higher Power, help me realize each day
that it is okay to be wrong,
that real communication with other
people depends on my being willing to see
other points of view, and that being
teachable is a divine quality.

Today I will handle being wrong by

God help me to stay clean and sober today!

JANUARY 6

Accepting powerlessness

There is nothing negative in the First Step of the program, where we admit that we are powerless over our addiction and our lives. Powerlessness is not weakness; it simply recognizes that power is an attribute of God, not humans.

We are powerless in and of ourselves. But when we look to the one who has all power, we can be set free—no longer bound by an addiction that does not love us. Have I tapped the source of all power?

Higher Power, help me to joyfully accept my powerlessness over my addiction, knowing that this will set me free.

I will accept my powerlessness today by

God help me to stay clean and sober today!

JANUARY 7

Finding balance

Let's not forget to play. Our new way of life is a serious matter, but it is not intended as a punishment; nor do we need to repent and suffer for the rest of our lives. Our new way of life is intended to produce growth.

But growth takes work. And work needs play for balance. If we forget to play and be joyful, our life will become unbalanced and we will suffer needlessly.

Have I found some balance in my life?

Higher Power, help me remember
that all living things need balance:
let me laugh, let me play, let me grow.

My plan for playing today is

God help me to stay clean and sober today!

JANUARY 8

Dealing with anger

Anger has its place, but chemically dependent people tend to let anger run away with them. The old saying "Be angry, but sin not" is a tall order for us. Two sins of anger are revenge and resentment. Either of them mixed with anger has a way of poisoning the angry one, both mentally and spiritually.

Since revenge and resentment are killers for us, it is best to turn over to our Higher Power the situations and people we are angry with.

How do I deal with my anger?

When I feel angry, whether justified or not, I pray that I keep it in check and turn it over.

Today I will deal with my anger
constructively by

God help me to stay clean and sober today!

JANUARY 9

Changing

You cannot build a house or a life without some foundation. While we were still drinking or using drugs, it seemed our lives could not change. *There was no foundation to build on.* We had no working principles in our lives. We found we could not become the good things we wanted to become.

Until we quit drinking or using, we didn't know that there was a way we could make ourselves, one day at a time, into the kind of person we could accept. But the Steps and the fellowship make personality change possible.

How have I changed?

Higher Power, let me be willing to love myself and live myself into a new life, one day at a time, based on honesty, open-mindedness, and willingness.

I will seek change today by

God help me to stay clean and sober today!

JANUARY 10

Seeking growth

We are where we are for a reason. As long as that reason remains, we remain where we are. If we aren't where we think we should be, working the program will help us get to where our deepest self longs to be. This is growth.

And growth is work. We must be willing to do the simple things that our new understanding asks of us. We are never given more than we can handle, and the loving help we need along the way is always available. But we never get this help in advance, only as we need it.

Am I seeking growth?

Higher Power, help me want to grow
and be willing to do the simple things,
day by day, that add up to big changes.

I will seek growth today by

God help me to stay clean and sober today!

JANUARY 11

Enjoying reality

Cloud Nine does not compare to the joys and beauty of a clean life. In fact, Cloud Nine is opposed to our new way of life. It's a fantasy, a trip, a high—like that first drink, fix, or pill.

Now we are dealing with reality—a real and beautiful place instead of a fanciful dream. Each day can be a journey with our Higher Power, beyond pain and suffering, beyond Cloud Nine, in the wonderful here and now.

Am I learning to enjoy today?

I pray for guidance
through all aspects of growing,
so I don't get stuck in any one place.

The real things I will enjoy today are

God help me to stay clean and sober today!

JANUARY 12

Changing our attitudes

Our prayer is, "God, grant me the serenity to accept the things I cannot change, courage to change the things I can, and the wisdom to know the difference." We say this prayer at least once a day because although we must accept the things we cannot change today, they may, in fact, change tomorrow.

This seems to be a paradox, yet once we truly and completely accept something, it begins to change. While the objective fact remains unchanged, our attitude toward it and our relationship to it has changed. It is with our attitudes toward people and things that we must learn to live.

Am I changing my attitudes?

Higher Power, help me live fully today,
neither forward nor backward,
but here and now.

The attitude I will work on today is

God help me to stay clean and sober today!

Seeing the beauty

We can see our Higher Power in so many beautiful things in this world: the reflection of light in the running brook; the spectrum of colors in the oil spot on the street; the stubbly grass peeking out of the snow like morning whiskers; hail popping like kernels of corn; the music of rain; the face of a child; the face of an elder.

Some of us see our Higher Power most clearly in the light of another's eyes or in acts of unselfish kindness and know ourselves to be part of it. With clean, sober eyes we can see this beauty.

Can I see the beauty all around me?

Higher Power, help me see the beauty all around me today and to realize that I, too, am beautiful in your eyes.

Today I will look for the beauty in

God help me to stay clean and sober today!

JANUARY 14

Being true

We believe we can become beautiful people, free of addiction. With belief in a Power greater than ourselves, our Twelve Step program, and the fellowship, we don't have to stay where we were. Our purpose in life is to stay sober and clean.

Our Higher Power knows our true purpose in life and will help us. Our Higher Power knows what we are capable of becoming, although others may misjudge us.

Am I staying true to my purpose?

I pray that I may see the good within me
and remain true to my purpose.

I will honor my true purpose today by

God help me to stay clean and sober today!

Sharing feelings

Many of us just did what other people did: We took drugs. But we felt so different from "normal" people. Why? Because of the way we did drugs and because drugs were so unfulfilling for us. It's a joke among us recovering addicts that we tried so hard to look normal.

Nonaddicts didn't know our torment, didn't know that we lived in another world. While high, we felt moments of euphoria and false well-being. When the drugs wore off, we suffered centuries of misery. Both are feelings that "normal" people did not experience.

In the fellowship, however, we share all our feelings because we know that we are among friends, we know that we are finally home.

Do I share my true feelings with others?

Higher Power, I pray for the willingness to see my true feelings more clearly and to share myself with my fellow addicts.

The feelings I will share today are

God help me to stay clean and sober today!

JANUARY 16

Sharing our sobriety

We cannot give away something we don't have. And since the people closest to us forced us to see our inadequacies, our inability to love, most of us resented them. Although aware of the problem, we hated having it shown to us regularly. We were empty and scared. And there was no hope in sight, so we blamed our problems on those around us.

But by coming into the program things change: First we get hope; then we get strength and experience to share with other alcoholics and nonalcoholics. We learn that in order to keep what we've been given so freely, we must give it away.

Do I share my sobriety with others?

Higher Power, help me be ever aware of the source of all the good things I've been given, and show me each day how to share them with others.

Today I will share my sobriety with

God help me to stay clean and sober today!

JANUARY 17

Accepting our limitations

Helen Keller said, "Life is a banquet and most of us are starving to death." Drinking and using sure kept us from seeing the beauty, the bounty in our lives. Since we recognized that we can't use or drink—and got clean and sober—most of us today can get higher than ever before on the important things like justice, peace, and love.

Those of us who seem successful in relationships have at some point learned to accept our shortcomings more than most.

Am I learning to accept my limitations?

> Higher Power, help me accept myself today, with all my defects, knowing that in your time I will gradually change for the better.

The personal limitations I accept today are

God help me to stay clean and sober today!

JANUARY 18

Listening well

Learning to really listen to another human being—beyond just his or her words—is critical to good communication. Valuable exchanges between human beings can occur only when each listens carefully to the other and tries sincerely to understand the other person's meaning. Much anger and frustration with others could be avoided if we truly understood one another.

Constant thoughts running through our minds is a form of talking, and we can't listen to another (including our Higher Power) if we are still talking.

Do I really listen?

Higher Power, help me be quiet enough
within to listen to others today.
By trying to understand another,
let me learn something about myself.

Today I will quiet my mind and really listen to

God help me to stay clean and sober today!

JANUARY 19

Taking it easy

Easy does it. Pushing does not help our program; it only causes more pressure within us. "If it doesn't work," we have thought, "get a bigger hammer." But if we only wait for the opportunity, we will be given the opportunity to work out each of our difficulties.

It is better to work out a problem by taking two steps forward and one step back, rather than to push and try to solve it at once, fail, and then stop trying. It helps to remember that we are never given more than we can handle, one day at a time.

Have I learned to take it easy?

Higher Power, I depend on you for my very breath. Help me realize that the more I depend on you, the more I accept your help, the more I can handle.

I will take it easy today by

God help me to stay clean and sober today!

Avoiding blame

It is not uncommon to hear in group, "Why do these things always happen to me?" If these things are *always* happening to us, the obvious answer is that we somehow bring them on ourselves. We are largely unconscious of what we're doing (wrong) until, slowly, eventually, we manage to dig ourselves out from the results. (It seems incredible that we actually seek to be hurt, but in a way many of us do so, with regularity.)

But blaming others for our problems and indulging in self-pity don't move us along in our program.

Am I still blaming others?

Higher Power, help me take responsibility for myself and my actions, because blaming others will only keep me stuck.

I will take greater responsibility for myself today by

God help me to stay clean and sober today!

Keeping our motives honest

Motives are important in dealing with other people. If we're frank with someone and that person gets upset, we might think he or she just can't handle our directness, our honesty. But "honesty" without love is more like brutal frankness. If we want to be confrontational, we have to put up with the consequences.

But what is the real reason for being confrontational ("honest"), for pointing out others' flaws? Are we perhaps afraid that our own flaws will be discovered? Are we protecting ourselves by focusing attention on others?

Are my motives always honest?

Higher Power, help me see where
my motives are selfish or mean or petty,
so that I stay honest in my program.

Today I will examine my motives concerning

God help me to stay clean and sober today!

Accepting the past

Noted psychiatrist Carl Jung once said, "If one can accept one's sin, one can live with it. If one cannot accept it, one has to suffer the inevitable consequences." We must come to accept our past acts before they will stop causing us pain.

All the Steps help us do this, but in particular, Steps Four and Five (the inventory Steps) and Steps Eight and Nine (the amends Steps) help. If we attend to these Steps properly, we will no longer regret the past nor wish to shut the door on it.

Am I coming to accept myself?

Higher Power, help me accept the ways I've behaved in the past—and the ways I behave in the present—that cause me pain, so that in your time I may be freed.

I will work on self-acceptance today by

God help me to stay clean and sober today!

Letting others do it themselves

Our new way of life is a *self*-development program. Each person must do it for himself or herself. Sometimes an eager newcomer falls away when he or she discovers that there are no magic wands, only hard work in spiritual and emotional development.

But we can't heal the world of addiction. We can't shove our cherished new ideals down anyone's throat (but we can hold out a hand when they decide they want to get well).

Do I let others do it for themselves?

> Higher Power, may I realize that it
> "took what it took" for me and that
> it will be the same for others.

*Today I will decide on these three personal
boundaries for helping newcomers*

God help me to stay clean and sober today!

Getting honest

Most of us have tried to con ourselves into believing that maybe it was actually okay for us to use drugs, because we needed an occasional tension reliever, for example. When we said that, we were still considering drugs as our Higher Power.

We approached the question *Why not use drugs?* from every angle, hoping that we could win the argument and rationalize using. When we get honest about *Why not?* we begin to accept our condition.

Am I honest about my true condition?

> Higher Power, help me accept that
> I am mentally and physically different
> from nonaddicts, so that I can be
> free of the desire to use chemicals.

I will be honest about my condition today by

God help me to stay clean and sober today!

Being open

Sometimes we think we're supposed to have more recovery under our belts. Perhaps we feel the need to impress our peers with our success in staying off mind-altering chemicals. But perhaps we are really just trying to convince ourselves. We know how difficult recovery is, and surely our Higher Power is not fooled by our pretense of well-being.

If we try to hide our problems, we cannot get help for them. To get help we must tell people where we're really at. No one can read a closed book.

Am I open with others?

> Higher Power, help me believe in the saying, "Ask and you shall receive."

Today I will be more open and honest about

God help me to stay clean and sober today!

Embracing virtues and new attitudes

Because of our addiction, our actions (and inaction) have fostered cynicism, futility, and distrust. How could we ever have hoped to succeed with attitudes like that?

Now we are cultivating the virtues of understanding, love, and patience. It is often slow and difficult. We know that our Higher Power loves us and will lead us, if we only ask.

Am I developing new virtues?

Higher Power, take my hand and lead me from the old attitudes toward new virtues.

I will work on the following virtues today

God help me to stay clean and sober today!

Finding joy

In the revelation of life (not in booze, pills, or junk) our first joy is the very fact that we are alive. Next, we find gladness and joy in our daily activities and accomplishments.

Soon we discover the joy of service to others. Later our happiness widens when we learn to share the joys of our brothers and sisters. And finally, we find joy in our Higher Power.

Am I finding joy?

Higher Power, may I experience joy in the world around me, joy in being myself.

Today I will look for the joy in

God help me to stay clean and sober today!

Believing in change

At first, drugs or booze turned us on; later they turned on us. We couldn't find any peace anywhere. We began turning into the kind of person we didn't want to be, but we didn't know what was happening to us or how to change.

When we came to believe that our lives could and would turn around if we quit drinking or using, things began to get better.

Do I believe I can change?

Higher Power, help me to be open-minded
and humble enough to believe that
what has worked to change the lives
of others will work to change mine.

Today I will seek change by

God help me to stay clean and sober today!

JANUARY 29

Letting go of fear

Those of us who have been sober and clean for a period of time share newcomers' concerns for the future, but we do not share their fear. We know how unsafe they feel, but we know how safe they are. The richness of life is often overlooked by giving minor events too much attention.

By working the Steps, going to meetings, and sharing in the fellowship—the newcomer will learn to relax. The newcomer will feel the richness of life and lose his or her fear by working the program and staying clean and sober.

Am I losing my fear?

Higher Power, help me let go of my fear
so that I can be ready to experience
the richness of life as it comes my way.

Today I will combat my fear by

God help me to stay clean and sober today!

JANUARY 30
Taking it slowly

Let's not make haste and demand perfection at once—this would only blind us. If we are impatient, we cannot work a daily program. But by exercising patience, we learn to recognize daily opportunities for growth.

It is worth waiting for, striving for, and working to develop a relationship with our Higher Power. It cannot be done overnight. Let's not go too fast, but count each day as a new opportunity.

Am I learning to take it slowly?

Higher Power, I pray that I may meet each day with patience and grow closer to you.

I will take it easy today by

God help me to stay clean and sober today!

JANUARY 31

Living new lives

If we thank our Higher Power each day for the problems in our lives, we will find that we can live and cope with them. And if it is our Higher Power's will, our problems will be transformed in ways we cannot comprehend. We don't fully understand our lives.

If we become willing to let our Higher Power handle each situation in its way, we will see that we are living ourselves into new ways of being. We will experience a freedom and joy that we could not have understood in our old ways of thinking and being.

We cannot think ourselves into a better life; we must live ourselves each day into better thinking.

Am I living myself into a new life?

Higher Power, I am grateful
for the problems in my life; they help me
change myself into a new being.

*Today I will live myself into a
new way of thinking about*

God help me to stay clean and sober today!

FEBRUARY 1

Doing our best

Perhaps we are saving our best effort for the "big break." *When such and such happens, then I'll give it my best shot.* What we don't realize, however, is that success comes from doing a lot of little things well. Learning to live means learning to manage all our daily responsibilities.

If we can't keep our clothes clean, take out the garbage, or get up on time, how can we expect to handle promotions, marriages, and crises? Daily effort may seem inconsequential, but our big break is the result of all our todays well lived.

Do I always give my best effort?

> Higher Power, help me take care
> of each thing as it comes along.

Today I will do my best when I

God help me to stay clean and sober today!

FEBRUARY 2

Learning patience

Many of us spent a long time getting sick, and we can't expect to recover overnight. We have to want to get well, and we must be patient. If we lose control through lack of patience, we may lose all that we've gained.

Patience is a slowly developing virtue. It requires that we watch ourselves each day and use prayer in trying times. (Being selfish, however, retards our progress.)

Am I developing patience?

Higher Power, help me learn patience
in living the life set before me.

I will practice patience today by

God help me to stay clean and sober today!

FEBRUARY 3

Practicing what we know

Our Higher Power does not expect us to live what we do not know or do not yet understand. But we can gain understanding by applying what we know day by day. (When we turn our backs on what we already know, then we stumble.)

We already know that drinking and using only block our way. When should we begin applying what we already know? *Today.* For today is the *only* day we have.

Do I practice what I know?

Higher Power, help me apply what I know
and not turn my back on my
program of recovery.

I will practice what I know today by

God help me to stay clean and sober today!

Carrying the message

When first we experience the joys and blessings of this program, many of us are filled
with a fever to carry the message and do
God's work. We absorb some spiritual principles and grow elated at the prospect of our
do-gooding! At this point vanity becomes a
danger. We may feel that we, above others,
are true messengers of God. Perhaps we are
even tempted to start preaching *the* way to
spiritual growth. What vanity!

God works through everyone—not just a
select few. God even works through the failure of others, to remind us of our past. None
of us knows *the* way, for God has provided
many ways.

How do I carry the message?

As I do my work today, may I know that
all of us are from God and all are
returning to God, and none of us
is more beautiful than the next.

*Today I will humbly try to
show others the way by*

God help me to stay clean and sober today!

Imitating

We don't need to imitate anyone. If we admire someone, we might aspire to her or his qualities (substance), but we needn't imitate that person's every gesture and word (style). A person's talent is the sum of his or her experiences; we can't simply adopt them. And we don't need to! Our Higher Power will teach us what we have to offer.

We don't know our capabilities—nor do others—until we have exhibited them. When we do what we are asked to do, to the best of our ability, we feel a moment of great joy and fulfillment. No matter how small the task, we are then right in the eyes of God.

Have I stopped imitating?

Higher Power, I pray for your presence
in all areas of my life and your
guidance in all I do.

I will practice being my best self today by

God help me to stay clean and sober today!

FEBRUARY 6

Seeing the good

The beauty of our souls shines in many ways: The greatest of these is love. In the spirit of loving kindness, every day a little ugliness is removed; our perspective on life grows broader and deeper.

In the spirit of love, our lives become fresher, our souls humbler; evil seems to disappear, and we learn to distinguish sinner from the sin.

Do I see the good in people?

Higher Power, let me walk in your love
and see the good in all things.

Today I will look for the good in

God help me to stay clean and sober today!

Avoiding compulsiveness

Being compulsive people, once we leave the alcohol and other drugs behind, we want our dreams fulfilled *now*. But when we first get into recovery, all we have is potential. Fulfillment is not realized immediately; rather it is something we work toward.

Each day we must work on our lives with what we know today. Gradually we will grow closer toward our ideal. (Recovery is a process.) But we won't get anywhere if we try forcing ourselves into situations we are not ready for. God sets the pace.

Have I stopped being compulsive?

**Higher Power, I pray for the patience
to live today with what I have
and what I know.**

I will avoid being compulsive today by

God help me to stay clean and sober today!

Expressing love

As we recover, we come to realize the presence of a Higher Power in our lives. Eventually we realize how much progress in recovery comes through our Higher Power. We realize that we are loved.

Being loved, we can love others, but we cannot love mankind until we love our God. And we cannot love our God until we love each other. (And we cannot love each other until we love ourselves.)

When we practice loving our fellows (in thought, word, and deed), we feel the presence of our Higher Power and feel that we, too, are loved.

Do I express my love for others?

**Higher Power, help me recognize
your presence and power in my life.
Help me love others as I am loved.**

I will show my love for others today by

God help me to stay clean and sober today!

Remembering our powerlessness

If we've been around so long that we think our bad times are over and we can't get "crazy" again, then we probably have already gotten "crazy" in the head. None of us is immune to relapse nor so spiritual that we have no room for improvement. If we think we no longer need help, we may be in trouble already.

If we have forgotten our powerlessness, we may have to learn it all over again. As addicts, we will always be at risk to relapse, but with proper guidance we can be productive and fulfilled.

Do I realize how powerless and at risk I truly am?

Higher Power, I take pride and joy
in being clean and sober,
but help me remember how powerless
I still am and keep me humble.

*I will remind myself of my powerlessness
today by*

God help me to stay clean and sober today!

Praying for things

It seems that in our selfishness we're always praying for the things that we want and not the things we need. If we pray for and receive luxury, sexual fulfillment, or an easy life, what do we gain? Certainly not strength, wisdom, and love.

To gain strength we must carry burdens; to gain wisdom we must become honest with ourselves; and to gain love we must become loving. These virtues are not accomplished through material things, sex, or a soft life.

Am I praying for the right things?

> Higher Power, help me pray for the right things and to accept that you will give me what I need and not necessarily what I want.

Today I will pray for

God help me to stay clean and sober today!

Avoiding procrastination

In the midst of our addiction, everything could be put off, including people: We had to have our stuff.

Now that we have the business of life to tend to—now that we *have* a life—are we doing what we need to today? Or are we putting things off until tomorrow? If we don't take care of business today, we could relapse and lose what we have gained from the Twelve Steps and the fellowship.

Have I stopped procrastinating?

Higher Power, help me do what I need to do today; help me persevere to prevent losing what I have gained.

Today I will do three things that I have been putting off; they are

God help me to stay clean and sober today!

Living today

Sometimes we expect so much so fast that we become nervous wrecks. Expecting answers for tomorrow's or next week's problem is not living today.

If we have a problem today, let us retake the Third Step, offer the problem to our Higher Power for an answer, and practice patience with the future.

Can I work on just today's problem?

Higher Power, help me live
one day at a time and to accept
your answers when you send them.

My plan for working on today's problem is

God help me to stay clean and sober today!

FEBRUARY 13

Solving problems

If we start the morning feeling hopeless, our day doesn't stand a chance. But if we ask our Higher Power for help in the morning and then accept the help throughout the day, we won't have to solve any problems alone.

We will see that problems can be resolved, and we are responsible only for our efforts.

Do I leave the solutions to God?

Higher Power, grant me the strength to ask for help and simply to do my part well.

Today I will work on three problems and leave the solutions to God. The problems are

God help me to stay clean and sober today!

FEBRUARY 14

Learning that God is love

"God is love." Through love our lives can be made whole. If we love ourselves, we don't abuse our bodies with alcohol and other drugs. If we love ourselves, we don't mistreat our minds with hate. If we love ourselves, we don't treat our fellows unkindly.

When we truly know that God is love—a love that includes suffering and pain as well as splendor and light—we need never be alone in despair again.

Do I know God is love?

Higher Power, I pray that I may know
the meaning and power of your love.

I will seek to know God's love today by

God help me to stay clean and sober today!

FEBRUARY 15

Overcoming barriers

When situations seem the darkest, the storm may be about to break up and let the sun shine through. A bit more persistence, a bit more effort, and the emotional turmoil that seemed hopeless may resolve into a process of growth. All battles, whether won or lost, are internal.

God never places impossible barriers in front of us; our barriers are only those we create for ourselves.

Am I still erecting barriers against my own progress?

Higher Power, grant me the strength
to carry on my internal struggles.

*Today I will work on
bringing down barriers by*

God help me to stay clean and sober today!

FEBRUARY 16

Being kind

Saying an unkind word to another may not hurt that person the rest of his or her life, but what does it do to us? It separates us from our spiritual fellowship, which we cannot afford.

It is when we are out of step, out of harmony, that we are vulnerable to taking that first fix, drink, or pill. So it will help us all to be kind to others (even to those who don't seem to appreciate it).

Am I kind to others?

Higher Power, help me show kindness
to all my brothers and sisters,
even when it is difficult,
as you have shown kindness to me.

I will show kindness today by

God help me to stay clean and sober today!

FEBRUARY 17

Taking care of today

If we want to be free of chemicals, then we must begin making changes right where we are today. Idly wishing for the past to be removed or the future to come closer gets us nothing. We must focus on today to make possible a better tomorrow.

This requires a clear understanding of what we can and cannot do today. So let us not distress ourselves by dwelling in the past or future, but express ourselves to the fullest today.

Have I learned to take care of today?

Higher Power guide me in my activities
today and keep me from dwelling
on the past or the future.

I will take care of today by

God help me to stay clean and sober today!

FEBRUARY 18

Praying by acting

There is more to prayer than just kneeling at night and folding our hands. Thoughts of love can be prayers. Feelings of gratitude can be prayers. Prayers can be seen in a smile, a gesture, and even an action not done.

Joy surging through our bodies is a prayer. Caring for a child is a form of prayer. Many times, no matter what the position of our bodies, our soul is on its knees.

Do I express prayer in all that I do?

Higher Power, help me pray throughout the day, knowing that your goodness abounds in me.

Today I will make prayers of my actions by

God help me to stay clean and sober today!

Practicing HALT

The acronym HALT means never get too Hungry, too Angry, too Lonely, or too Tired. Each of these conditions can fog our minds so that we lose sight of our purpose—abstinence and recovery—and have a slip.

If we can become more aware of our thoughts and feelings, we will avoid some pain and some slips. HALT is a good slogan to keep in mind.

Do I practice HALT?

> Higher Power, help me slow down
> and become more self-aware.

*Today when I feel myself getting hungry,
angry, lonely, or tired, I will*

God help me to stay clean and sober today!

FEBRUARY 20

Having realistic expectations

Sometimes we expect much too much of people and things. We will never be happy if we expect our doctor to work instant cures or if we blame our teacher for what we failed to learn. We need to examine what's realistic to expect of others and what we are responsible for ourselves. It's the same with the program: We cannot judge its effectiveness by whether we are happy all the time.

The program will be perfect only when we are perfect. We must let go of our childish all-or-nothing attitude and become more realistic. After all, when were we ever happy *all* the time?

Do I expect too much?

Higher Power, when I am unhappy
with the program, help me be honest
with myself about where the problem lies.

Today I will examine my expectations about

God help me to stay clean and sober today!

Becoming free

Many of us have said, "I want the freedom to be who I am." Do we realize, however, that our freedom is only as broad as the freedom we grant others? The more we let someone else be who he or she is, the more freedom we have to be ourselves.

Other people—people who are different from us—are mirrors for us. They can help us see what we're doing well or poorly; but more than that, they can be models for us and show us the way.

Am I becoming free?

Higher Power, help me learn
the valuable lessons of diversity.

*I will work on freedom today
by acknowledging the differences
between myself and
(name two people)*

God help me to stay clean and sober today!

FEBRUARY 22

Taking the Steps

We used drugs for many reasons. Often it was to take the edge off life. In the beginning drugs made the world more beautiful, more satisfying. Toward the end we used drugs to turn off our guilt, fear, and loneliness. The drugs began to cause more problems than they cured. Finally, using met none of our needs at all.

By working the Steps, however, we can learn to meet our needs in constructive, rather than destructive, ways.

Am I working all the Steps necessary to meet my needs without chemicals?

Higher Power, help me find those things in life—sober and clean—that I was trying to find by using drugs.

Today I will work on Step

God help me to stay clean and sober today!

FEBRUARY 23

Being sick and tired

We get sick and tired of blaming others for our faults. We get sick and tired of running the show. We get sick and tired of trying to impress people. *We are sick and tired of being sick and tired.*

We need only remember that when anything gets to be too much, when we get sick and tired of anything, God is always ready to help to take it from us.

Am I feeling sick and tired about anything now?

Higher Power, help me turn things over to you before I get that sick and tired feeling.

*Today I will ask my Higher Power
to take over two problems.
They are*

God help me to stay clean and sober today!

FEBRUARY 24

Being grateful

We grow in gratitude for the pure gift of being clean and sober. In time, we recognize and are grateful for its benefits.

The benefits we appreciate are many, including mended relationships with family and friends, the ability to sustain honesty in relationships, the awareness of our lives and our health, the ability to ask for help and to help others.

Am I grateful?

Higher Power, help me to be grateful
each day for just being sober and clean
and for the many blessings that brings.

I will express my gratitude today by

God help me to stay clean and sober today!

Holding on and letting go

We had a great deal of tenacity, except that we were holding on to destructive behaviors and attitudes: resentments and self-pity, drugs and other bad habits.

We must reassign this tenacity to what is realistic and what sustains us in life, then hold on carefully (like holding a newborn kitten).

Am I holding on to more of the good things?

> Higher Power, help me let go of
> the fear that keeps me from
> letting go of my defects.

The good things I will hold on to today are

God help me to stay clean and sober today!

FEBRUARY 26

Learning to live

Just as we learn to walk or talk, we must learn to live, day by day. When we got clean and sober, we had to learn how to live all over again. (Judging by our past we had not done so well in this area.)

If our desire is strong enough, God will take our hand and lead us step by step, day by day, into our new life. In time we will become the loving, mature adults we could not be for so many years before.

Am I learning to live?

> Higher Power, help me let go of
> my will and follow yours.

I will work on learning to live today by

God help me to stay clean and sober today!

Avoiding fights

The program encourages us to stop fighting against people and things. In fighting, our principles get blurred and it gets harder to think, so we have trouble doing what we know is right. In fighting, our center is anywhere but with our Higher Power.

To reduce change, it is more effective to show people your way rather than beat them into submission. Fighting is one approach; there are others. God will show us how to handle all situations.

Have I stopped fighting?

> Higher Power, help me learn new approaches to conflict and to trust in your help with new situations.

The one person or one thing I will stop fighting today is

God help me to stay clean and sober today!

Becoming open-minded

When we first came into this beloved fellowship, some of us felt that members were narrow-minded and so it would be hard to make friends. But that was just our fear and projection talking. How many fellowships embrace members of such varied backgrounds (age, race, occupation, and income)?

Most of us had much more limited contacts before we joined the fellowship. Now, as we become less narrow-minded, we lose some of our fear and discover some very open-minded people in this fellowship.

Am I becoming more open-minded?

Higher Power, help me accept and embrace the fact that I was led to this fellowship because I truly needed help.

Today I will practice being open-minded by

God help me to stay clean and sober today!

MARCH 1

Becoming vulnerable

When we choose not to escape through that first drink, fix, or pill, we are refusing to choose death. We are trusting that life can be interesting, life can be worthwhile, life can be *more* than it ever was before. Had we no hope of this, we never would have stopped using.

In one way we have been losers. To finally give life an honest try is to become vulnerable. (*Is there really a Higher Power who looks out for me?*)

And while we know the program works, we aren't sure if we are willing to risk working it. But it is only through taking this risk, and becoming vulnerable, that our life will ever "open up."

Do I dare become vulnerable?

Higher Power, grant me the courage
to give life an honest try.

I will risk being vulnerable today by

God help me to stay clean and sober today!

MARCH 2

Trusting my Higher Power

We know that other people, jobs, and new places could not relieve us of our addiction. Then where does our hope lie?

The God of our understanding can give us freedom from addiction if only we will admit our problems and accept help.

Am I trusting my Higher Power?

Higher Power, let nothing from the past stop me from trusting you.

I will deepen my trust in God today by

God help me to stay clean and sober today!

Experiencing growth

It is not easy to stay clean and sober. It takes all the strength we have. We may suffer mentally or physically, but now we can learn from our experiences. In our using days, we could suffer the same experience many times and not learn a thing.

Now we are facing life for the first time, and we have the chance to grow through our experiences. If we take that first pill, fix, or drink, we halt our chances of growing.

Am I growing from each new experience?

I pray for the strength to endure and
for the ability to grow through
each life experience without that
first fix, pill, or drink.

I will strengthen my abstinence today by

God help me to stay clean and sober today!

Reaching a balance with sex

Sex has always been a problem for us in one way or another. Some of us had too much, some too little; some were immoral and some prudish about the whole thing. As with other areas of our lives, we need to be realistic about sex and learn to reach a balance with ourselves.

Taking "chastity vows" and "letting it all hang out" are both a little extreme. We find that the balance must be ours—not an institution's or another's views.

Have I found my balance with sex?

Lord, help me see that my attitude toward sex is between my Higher Power and me and not based on the views of others.

Today I will seek a better balance with sex by

God help me to stay clean and sober today!

Finding happiness within

When we were taking drugs, we were looking for fulfillment and happiness. We couldn't face the reality of life, so we tried to create a world that we could feel comfortable in. We searched for our pleasures in sources outside ourselves, in people, places, and things.

In working our spiritual program we come to realize that happiness and contentment are to be found within. Gradually we become aware of our achievements and the beginning of gratitude slowly sets in. Little by little, the peace, pleasure, and happiness within grow, and then we can reach out and say, "Hey life, here I am!"

Am I full of inner peace and happiness?

I pray I may always remember that peace and happiness come from my Higher Power and that I may be grateful for it.

Today I will express gratitude for my inner peace and happiness by

God help me to stay clean and sober today!

MARCH 6

Feeling desperate

When we were drinking and using chemicals, we became accustomed to waking up to a feeling of impending doom, that desperate feeling of "What did I do or say yesterday?" and "What did people think?"

Even though we've quit using drugs or alcohol, sometimes, even after a good day, many of us continue to experience this feeling. It is a bad habit that is gradually eliminated simply by time and by rationally thinking over the previous day.

Am I learning to handle such feelings of desperation?

Higher Power, help me feel enough peace of mind to look at things rationally and to help me avoid being led into feelings of desperation by old habits.

If I feel desperate today, I will handle it by

God help me to stay clean and sober today!

MARCH 7

Accepting God's love

God's love is so encompassing and powerful that we cannot understand it. Doubtless, many have turned away from our fellowship because they could not accept such love. *Why would anyone want to love me? What's in it for them?*

Maybe these words were once ours, but as we apply our newfound principles we come to understand love, not in our intellect, but in our being. It is through the love and grace of our Higher Power that we have gained so much.

Am I accepting God's love?

Higher Power, may I come to know
the influence of your love, helping me
day by day, hour by hour.

Today I will accept God's love from

God help me to stay clean and sober today!

Going to any lengths

Before we sought help, we became very ill—physically, mentally, and spiritually. We couldn't stand to look at ourselves in a mirror. We had to hit bottom before we could help ourselves. But when we did, we became ready to try anything, to go to any lengths.

We must never forget where we came from and in what condition we arrived. We must not forget that we are pill heads, drunks, and junkies. If we do forget, our willingness to "go to any lengths" will fade away.

Am I still willing to go to any lengths?

Higher Power, I pray that I may always remember where I came from and in what condition I arrived at this program.

The lengths I will go to today are

God help me to stay clean and sober today!

MARCH 9

Having a sponsor

Why do people in this program always suggest we get a sponsor? Doubtful people ask, "If I have the whole fellowship to turn to, why do I need a sponsor?" Considering the fact that we have tricky minds, the whole fellowship would give us too many answers.

If we didn't like one answer, we could go to another and then another until we got the answer we wanted. But this would be self-will run riot and contrary to turning our will over to the care of God. A sponsor can put a check on our self-will.

Do I have a sponsor?

Higher Power, may I learn not to operate on self-will and may my mind stay clear so that I don't play games with my life.

Today I will talk with my sponsor about

God help me to stay clean and sober today!

Exercising patience

To be patient means being willing to wait for fulfillment. We can head straight for our goal of becoming clean and sober, asking for patience as we pause for the stoplights along the way and wait.

If we refuse to wait and plunge ahead, we are sure to go the long way around and per- haps lose sight of our objective in the process. We must always keep in mind that our objective is a clean and sober way of thinking and living. We must have patience or our objective will slip away.

Do I exercise patience?

Higher Power, help me to do the things today that will make me ready. Help me to be willing to wait for the right things.

I will exercise patience today by

God help me to stay clean and sober today!

MARCH 11

Seeking happiness

Happiness is not a goal for us, it is the result of following the Twelve Steps. If we make happiness an object of pursuit, it will only lead us on a wild goose chase. We know this because whenever we sought happiness out of a bottle, needle, or pill, it always eluded us.

When we are following our true purpose, we often find the happiness we never dreamed possible staring us in the face. When we work the Steps, help others, and go to meetings, we can't help but have happiness presented to us. It is a result.

The sooner we stop seeking happiness for itself, the sooner we realize that it's the by-product of our new life.

Have I stopped chasing rainbows?

Higher Power, help me see happiness as the *result* of the way I live.

I will practice the program today by

MARCH 12

Believing in abstinence

When we came to the fellowship, some of us weren't sure that we were "addicts." We knew we were unhappy. We knew we drank and used drugs too much, but we didn't know whether we used chemicals too much because we were unhappy or whether we're unhappy because we used chemicals too much.

It was suggested to us that we try not using drugs along with working the Twelve Steps to see if our lives changed. They did! We have come to believe that there is no problem that taking a drink, fix, or pill will not make worse.

Am I convinced that abstinence is the only way?

> Higher Power, help me carry the message that if we simply don't take a drink, pill, or fix, our lives will change for the better.

Today I will carry the message of abstinence to

God help me to stay clean and sober today!

Changing our ways

We must be willing to grow in understanding. When we were using chemicals we understood everything in one way, a way that caused us pain and misery. When we quit drinking or using other drugs, we began to see things in another way.

This new way of seeing things means we've had to make some changes in our way of living, and any new way of thinking means new ways of being. Are we willing to make the changes in our living that correspond with our new ways of thinking?

Am I changing my ways of living?

Higher Power, give me the courage, belief, and willingness I need to allow change to take place in my life.

One way of living that I will change today is

God help me to stay clean and sober today!

MARCH 14

Making amends

There is no benefit in trying to make amends until we are entirely willing to do it. We must be ready to make our amends without preconceived ideas about how the other party will receive them.

The success of the amends Steps does not depend on the acceptance of the other party but merely on our total willingness to admit where we were wrong. There is magic in working the amends Steps, magic we can never believe in until we work them.

Have I made all of my amends?

Higher Power, help me to be willing to
ask forgiveness of you and to admit
my mistakes to those I have wronged.
Please remove my fear of doing so.

Today I will make amends to

God help me to stay clean and sober today!

MARCH 15

Living honestly

We can live ourselves into being new people as we act honestly in each situation, one by one. Each day, honestly lived to the depth of our ability, will result in new experiences, richer and fuller than the day before.

Unless we live our honesty, we are destined to stay in our old ruts. Being honest with ourselves and others creates many new opportunities for us.

Do I practice honesty in all of my affairs?

God, grant me the humility to be
honest with others today and the light
to be honest with myself.

I will cultivate self-honesty today by

God help me to stay clean and sober today!

Giving up possessiveness

Gradually we begin to see that everything belongs to God. As long as we strive to possess, we are not free. It is possible to simply use things without possessing them. Ownership is really only stewardship, and whatever is in our care must be used for the good.

But this doesn't mean we won't have what we need. If we first seek the spiritual in life, we will not go wanting, and we will discover that less is more.

Am I giving up my possessiveness?

Higher Power, help me to keep in mind that the air which sustains me is not mine.

Today I will select two of my possessions to give to charity; they are

God help me to stay clean and sober today!

Getting in touch with our feelings

When we were using alcohol and other drugs we lost our moral path. It caused us anguish to feel one way but act another. Eventually we got so confused that *we* wondered how we really felt.

But now in the program, we want to get honest with ourselves. We want to know our feelings and be able to express them. After a while, those around us will begin to feel that they can trust us and depend on us.

Can I reveal my true feelings?

> God, give me the courage to be
> honest with myself and others
> about how I am feeling,
> especially if it's not how I wish I felt.

The true feelings I will disclose today are

God help me to stay clean and sober today!

Freeing ourselves of judgments

Since we tend to condemn in others what we dislike in ourselves we must free ourselves of judgments. Since whatever we express reflects back on us, why express anything but love?

When we judge, condemn, and misunderstand, we invite judgment, condemnation, and misunderstanding in return.

Have I stopped judging others?

Higher Power, let me not judge others
today but express the love
that I am capable of giving.

Today I will express love to

God help me to stay clean and sober today!

Removing defects

Through working the Steps we can discover which of our character traits are valuable and which no longer work for us. And very, very gradually, as we grow in the program, we can let go of the traits that aren't working.

We have suffered much because of our imperfections. When we are ready to quit suffering, we will be willing to ask that these defects of character be removed, one at a time. When we are willing to work at them a day at a time, we will discover miraculous changes beginning to take place in ourselves.

Am I letting go of all my defects?

Higher Power, I am entirely ready and willing to have my defects of character removed.

The defect I will work on letting go of today is

Letting go of false pride

What's going on when we say that some things aren't good enough for us? Some of us feel that if we can't "win" at work, romance, or sports we won't even play. This is called false pride.

If we are operating with false pride, chances are we'll also refuse help from others, the very help that might save our lives. If we can't accept anything from anybody, how can we expect to recognize and receive God's big gifts for us? We need to work on false pride by accepting little things from others.

Am I letting go of false pride?

Higher Power, help me open up
so that I can accept things from others,
whether simple or grand.

Today I will work on my false pride by

God help me to stay clean and sober today!

Nurturing new growth

Spring is a time of new and beautiful growth. There can be growth for us, too. We have spent too long in the fall and winter of our lives, the mind-altering chemicals filtering the sunshine and fading the flowers. Finally, our lives appeared empty and dead.

But like earth at the end of winter, there is still life within us. And when we make the conditions suitable, using abstinence, patience, and love, our lives will again bring forth new growth.

Am I returning or preparing for new growth?

Higher Power, may I feel your love
shine down on me to help me grow.

I will prepare for new growth today by

God help me to stay clean and sober today!

MARCH 22

Being honest inside

All the answers we will ever need are available to us. Even though they seem to come from outside us—through other people—the answers are already inside us. We need only recognize them when they emerge. Something inside us hears the truth, and for a long time we pretend that we don't notice it. But then one day, we decide to get honest about how we really feel.

At that point we gain a bit of freedom. We begin to make progress when we become honest with ourselves about how we really feel. Our Higher Power can help us, but only if we present ourselves with humble honesty.

Am I honest with myself about how I really feel inside?

Higher Power, allow me to really feel today, even though I risk being vulnerable.

Today I will examine my true feelings about

God help me to stay clean and sober today!

Getting well

It is important to remember we have been gravely ill, emotionally, physically, and spiritually. To get well, we must work on all three areas. Getting sober and clean is only a first step, because addiction is only a *symptom* of the real illness.

Once clean and sober, we must learn how to live. And then we must learn to be aware of God's presence. Let us work on these changes, day by day, and the light of God's presence will shine forth in our lives.

Am I recovering emotionally, physically, and spiritually?

Higher Power, help me remember
that my addiction is just a symptom of my
emotional, physical, and spiritual illness.

I will work on my spiritual health today by

God help me to stay clean and sober today!

Forming new habits

We form habits and then these habits begin to form us. For so long we had such self-destructive ways of being: We were self-centered, angry, and critical people, and so we behaved selfishly, angrily, and judgmentally in the world.

To stay clean and sober we must develop new habits, new patterns of living. We must give up old hangouts, old friends, old attitudes, and ideas. It seems this is the only way to form new habits—for example, kindness, love, and honesty—on which our program is based.

What habits do I want to develop?

Higher Power, help me to form new habits
to replace the old ones that
nearly destroyed my life.

The new habit I will work on today is

God help me to stay clean and sober today!

MARCH 25

Experiencing change

In recovery, there are great upheavals. Just as our whole drug world is let go, so too are many of our old ideas. Many a premise of our lives will prove weak and unreliable.

The only thing unshakable is God. Though fundamental change is shattering, our Higher Power will guide us through.

Am I experiencing a great upheaval?

> Higher Power, help me to accept
> the need for change and to accept
> your help to endure it.

*The area of my life I will work
on changing today is*

God help me to stay clean and sober today!

Worshipping

What we worship says a lot about the direction of our lives. Whatever else we worshipped, eventually we worshipped our addiction—going to any length to obtain and use our drug of choice. In our new life, however, we are learning to worship a new spiritual Higher Power.

As we work our Twelve Step program and learn about our new Higher Power—one who offers us no guilt, shame, danger, or losses—it might help to look at how others are coming to understand their Higher Power. We can learn from their example, just as we teach others indirectly by our own example.

What are my actions saying now about the direction of my life?

Higher Power, help me to express
my developing and deepening beliefs.

I will express my love of God today by

God help me to stay clean and sober today!

MARCH 27

Accepting myself

Accepting myself means not having to be rich, famous, powerful, or even "good." It means not having to impress others. It means living authentically. It means being comfortable saying, "I don't know."

To be free from fear means that we can live as we choose; it means we don't have to *be* anything in particular. We can just be aware and accepting.

Do I feel free to be me?

Higher Power, help me to
accept myself just as I am.

I will practice accepting myself today by

God help me to stay clean and sober today!

Maturing

In terms of age, most of us are fifteen going on thirty or forty or fifty. People in the program have observed that members stopped growing emotionally about the time they started using mood-altering chemicals. It may sound funny, but these observations appear accurate. If we look around us, many newer members do seem stuck in their teenage years.

But abstinence, patience, and working the program help us mature to our proper ages. Given time, we can become the adults we have only pretended to be for so long.

Am I maturing?

Higher Power,
help me to grow emotionally.

I will act maturely today by

God help me to stay clean and sober today!

Smiling

It is not uncommon for people addicted to chemicals to want to get back at those who rejected them or hurt them. For many years we probably operated on the law of revenge, and there was no bad situation that we couldn't make worse. Now what is our guide?

Have we tried the law of kindness to see how it could affect our neighbor? A smile can raise hope, and hope is a haven for us all. Let us smile to bring hope.

Am I willing to smile?

Higher Power, help me accept myself and others—and help me smile.

Today, I will give a smile to all I meet, and especially to

Debating the program

In school we may have joined in debates. They went on and on, and nobody ever had any answers. In our personal training grounds, the world of the streets, we often heard or participated in lengthy debates about the evils of our society. Of course, nothing ever changed.

Some people get clean and sober and then start debating about the Twelve Steps. The "answers" come to those who live the program, but such debate is of little value.

Am I living the program?

God, grant me the courage to take action
and thus truly live the program.

Today I will put the Steps into action by

God help me to stay clean and sober today!

MARCH 31

Handling the little things

It is less the crises that damage our quality of life than the daily irritations. There is some recognition for handling the big crises, but who notices how we handle the little things?

There is no recognition for handling irritations, but instead, there is peace and serenity. When peace and serenity dominate our lives daily, we begin to appreciate the real gift of this program, the gift of daily living.

Am I learning to handle the little things?

God, grant me patience and perspective as I practice dealing with all the little things.

I will change how I handle irritations today by

God help me to stay clean and sober today!

APRIL 1

Changing our fate

Perhaps we feel that life has played a trick on us: Fate has made us different from other people. We are chemically dependent and may feel life has made fools out of us. If we really examine ourselves, however, we'll find it was not just life but our self-will that helped us get into trouble.

Most of our problems were of our own making, not something fate dealt out. The only remedy we know is to align our will with our Higher Power. We can choose not to be fools of fate.

Am I changing my fate?

I pray that I may take responsibility
for my recovery.

I will align my will to God's will today by

God help me to stay clean and sober today!

APRIL 2

Avoiding competition

In our using days, we needed to know who had what job, what house, what car, who made more money, and so on. Yet learning to turn our lives over to God is not a spiritual contest.

Our spiritual quest should be to carry out God's will for us. It should not be to spiritually outdo others. God knows our capabilities and gives us a place that we can suitably fill.

Have I stopped competing?

> May I stop competing and
> leave the measurement of this day
> to my Higher Power.

I will avoid competing today by

God help me to stay clean and sober today!

APRIL 3

Rediscovering love

We know that in each of us, a fountain of love lies buried ready to be discovered. If we practice our newfound principles and continue searching we'll uncover our treasure, little by little, beneath our resentments, unhealthy style, and shame.

Our Higher Power and the Twelve Step program give us the guidance, strength, and tools necessary to uncover it.

Am I finding love?

> Higher Power, help me use the tools
> you give me so that I may reconnect
> with my reservoir of love.

I will make myself open to love today by

God help me to stay clean and sober today!

APRIL 4

Working for peace of mind

To stay clear of mood-altering chemicals, we must keep our thoughts close to our Higher Power. If we stay close, we will know peace but not necessarily leisure.

The work of recovery is hard, but our rewards are many and much more lasting than the immediate gratification we sought in the past.

Am I finding peace of mind?

Higher Power, help me stay close
to you and remember why I must work
on my recovery.

*Three ways I can work for
peace of mind today are*

God help me to stay clean and sober today!

Unlearning old ways

In this program we are not asked so much to learn new ways as to unlearn our old ones. We are not asked so much to adjust to new values as to see the folly of our old ones. How we will live our new lives is between us and our Higher Power, and surely there is room for diversity.

We are not asked to adopt the lifestyles or thinking of fellow addicts; we are asked only to live with honesty, an open mind, and a willingness to learn. We all use the program for sobriety, but what sobriety and a spiritual program lead us to is individual.

Am I unlearning the futile old ways?

> Higher Power, may the way of life
> I am now living help me let go of
> old ways and grow closer to you.

The old habit I will work at releasing today is

God help me to stay clean and sober today!

Working the Steps

In the beginning the Steps were just a theory to us, an ideal. Somehow they were supposed to keep us clean and sober! Some of us probably thought we couldn't possibly work the Steps. (Others thought we'd worked them all in three days.)

But the Steps *are* just theory until we work them! It's when we apply them that the value of this program becomes apparent in our lives. We don't get results and *then* work the Steps; we first work the Steps, *then* get results.

Am I satisfied with the results I see?

Higher Power, help me to see
that results come from working
the Steps and staying close to you.

The Step I will work on today is

God help me to stay clean and sober today!

Turning it over

It is true that if we turn our wills and our lives over to God, our problems will be lifted. It is easier to speak this truth than to live it.

Looking back, we see that following our own will has caused serious problems in our lives. Let's give this truth a chance. Let's pray, meditate, listen, and believe.

Am I turning it over?

God, help me to stop holding on so tight
and to have faith.

Today I will turn my will over to God by

God help me to stay clean and sober today!

APRIL 8

Keeping it simple

Keep it simple. What seems complex in our minds may not be complex in reality. We may not really be in the mess we think we are in. Serenity is available today if we accept today as it is, setting aside both yesterday and tomorrow. If we do what we need to do today, we will be in harmony and at peace.

What we need to be doing "out there" is right here, right now; it is as close as our spouse, children, job, and fellows in recovery.

Am I keeping it simple?

Higher Power, help me let go of everything
that interferes with simply doing
what I need to be doing right now.

*I will simplify my life today by tending to
what is mine to do, right here, right now by*

God help me to stay clean and sober today!

APRIL 9

Rewriting the program

People who abuse mood-altering chemicals fall into three categories with respect to the Twelve Step program: those who neglect the program entirely, those who try to put the program right, and those who want the program to put them right. Needless to say, those in the first two categories do themselves little good.

If we expect to recover strictly on our own or feel the need to rewrite the Steps, arrogance and self-centeredness will block us every time. But when we accept the fact that something bigger than us can help, we are well on the road to recovery.

Am I living the program as prescribed?

Higher Power, help me believe that
if I can't, you can, and if I let you, you will.

I will practice accepting the program today by

God help me to stay clean and sober today!

Improving the way we feel

It is hard to see that we lay the groundwork for all our emotions. It's also hard to accept the fact that we tend to blame our pain on anything or anyone else. That way, we placed all responsibility outside ourselves.

We are the source of most of our troubles, but we can also be the source of our happiness. If we make conditions inside ourselves conducive to joy and happiness, joy and happiness will be a part of us as well. Through God, we can change the conditions inside ourselves.

How am I feeling inside?

Higher Power, help me to make
the conditions inside myself a place
for good things and not just troubles.

I will improve the way I feel today by

God help me to stay clean and sober today!

Being free

Some psychologists believe that some people don't want to be free. In the middle of our addiction, we certainly had no freedom. We lost it all to the call of that fix, pill, or drink. We lost our freedom because we lost the power to decide how we wanted to behave. We had no choice.

Now we have a choice, and although we can never be free from our addiction, we can be free *in* our addiction! We can never be a former alcoholic or an ex-addict, but never again must we take those chemicals and destroy our being. The choice is ours.

Am I choosing to be free?

> I pray to realize that if I let go
> and let God, I will be free.

I will honor my freedom today by

God help me to stay clean and sober today!

Accepting God's will

Step Eleven concludes, ". . . praying only for knowledge of His will for us and the power to carry that out." This tells us that when we pray for "whatever is right," the best will happen for all concerned, including ourselves. We may even receive more than we asked for.

In times of crisis, when we feel that things must go our way or we'll lose faith in God, do we stop to remember that God works in mysterious ways? Nothing, not even death, is without a purpose. Accepting whatever comes as God's will avoids blame and anger, and keeps us present and focused.

Am I learning acceptance?

> Higher Power, help me understand
> that disasters are not punishments,
> and they can make your purpose clear.

I will practice acceptance today by

God help me to stay clean and sober today!

Growing

We all perform on two stages, one public, one private. The public stage is what we do and say. The private stage is what we think and what we rehearse in our minds to do on the public stage. Even though we may never perform it, what we rehearse in our minds helps mold our characters and guide our actions.

Are we rehearsing anger, fights, and what we're going to tell that SOB next time? Are we rehearsing drug use, the old ways of living? If so, we are risking the recovery we have achieved.

To keep growing and to keep building character, we need to rehearse kindness, patience, and love. We need to practice awareness of our Higher Power in our lives.

Am I growing?

> May I practice kindness, patience, and love in all my affairs today.

Today I will seek to grow by

God help me to stay clean and sober today!

APRIL 14

Discovering beauty

When we were using drugs we had only artificial vision, artificial experiences. We did not care how beautiful life was around us; we cared only about getting high and staying high. Now, as we grow in awareness, we are like little children discovering the world all over again.

We find there is more excitement in each discovery we make than there ever was in any high. We find that this excitement is real and that it cannot be taken from us.

Am I rediscovering the world around me?

> Higher Power, I pray to stay clean
> and sober so that I can be present
> and fully aware.

Today I will look for the beauty in

God help me to stay clean and sober today!

APRIL 15

Relying on faith

With our newfound recovery, we may find ourselves facing new situations with confidence. Our confidence must be supported by faith, however.

When trials arise, we realize how powerless we are and our confidence may crumble. Only faith can rescue us. Confidence is mental and emotional; faith is spiritual. Let us examine ourselves and see whether we are relying on confidence or on faith.

Is my faith strong enough?

Higher Power, increase my faith and courage so that I may face life's trials.

I will seek to deepen my faith today by

God help me to stay clean and sober today!

APRIL 16

Working on our goals

Our goal of staying clean and sober is a good one. At the spiritual level it is clear, but at the practical level some of us lack a commitment to it. Some of us even believe that the program won't work for us.

Such a belief is only an excuse not to realize our goals. We must work hard to hang on to our goals when fear, selfishness, and lack of faith get in our way.

Am I working on my goals?

Higher Power, help my unbelief
so that I may understand you
on both a practical and a spiritual level.

The goals I will work on today are

God help me to stay clean and sober today!

APRIL 17

Struggling alone

Each of us is a struggling soul. We had to struggle with our addictions for some time before we found this program, and eventually each struggling soul must face the realities of life. If we face the trials of life alone, we will fall.

But if we make our will one with our Higher Power in the Third Step, nothing will be too much to bear. After taking this Step, we will realize that we are one with God and that we don't have to struggle alone any longer.

Am I still struggling alone?

> May I turn my will and my life
> over to my Higher Power.

> *The struggles I will ask God
> for help with today are*

God help me to stay clean and sober today!

APRIL 18

Doing the little things

Commonplace acts of kindness are a way to God even more than the grand and glorious acts. It is the everyday observance of what we know to be right that will lead us to our Higher Power. We must live up to what we know will sustain us in our drug-free lives.

With smiles, friendly words, and patience during trying times, we will slowly climb the steps of growth. It is harder to do the little things every day than to shine forth in a crisis, and nothing that we do or don't do goes unnoticed by our Higher Power.

Do I tend to the little things every day?

Higher Power, help me find satisfaction in doing the simple, common tasks.

Two little things I will tend to today are

God help me to stay clean and sober today!

Using today's tools

Are we becoming stuck in the "if onlys"? "If only I had more money." "If only I were more attractive." "If only my parents had listened to Dr. Spock." The "if onlys" will get us nowhere. We would do better to think about what we have to work with *today*.

Do we remember that we are fortunate just to be alive? Are we grateful that, one day at a time, we are clean and sober? Do we keep in mind that we have at our disposal the Twelve Step program and all its tools? When we dwell in the "if onlys," we get stuck in yesterday. But what we have to work with today are "today's tools," and if we use them well, we'll have no need for the "if onlys."

Am I using the tools I have today?

God, help me to recognize today's tools
and to become willing to use them.

The tools I will use today are

God help me to stay clean and sober today!

APRIL 20

Being willing

People often ask, "How does the program work?" The HOW of this program is Honesty, Open-mindedness, and Willingness. Often we must pray for willingness; sometimes we even have to pray to be willing to be willing!

We have very stubborn wills. If surrendered daily, however, they can accomplish much good for ourselves and others. Surely those who say "I will, I will" and don't are not as close to the heart of God as those who say "I will not," but do!

Am I really willing?

God, help me realize that to
do your will for me today, in however
small a way, I must let go of my own will.

I will practice willingness today by

God help me to stay clean and sober today!

Reflecting kindness and love

We alcoholics and addicts can be sensitive to the remarks of loved ones and friends—at times they seem unkind to us. Yet if we examine ourselves, we may see that we are the ones who are out of tune. Perhaps we have turned away from our Higher Power and stopped working our program.

It is important to realize that what we see in others often reflects what is within *ourselves*. If I am afraid, I will see fear in others. If I feel anxious, I will see anxiety in others. When we come to understand that turning back to our Higher Power and our program means getting back in tune, then we'll be much less sensitive and our reflection will be soft and loving.

What does my reflection look like?

Lord, help me to take personal inventory
and stay close to the program.

Today I will reflect kindness and love by

God help me to stay clean and sober today!

Repairing the damage

It really does not matter how much we used or drank. The important thing is what it was doing to us, how it was affecting our lives. The biggest cop-out for people with addiction has always been, "I'm not using as much as other people, so maybe I'm not chemically dependent."

We couldn't admit what using was doing to our lives, our families, and friends. It nearly destroyed us, but now we have a chance to repair the damage. If we are willing to accept ourselves and to turn our will and our lives over to our Higher Power, we can restore our lives.

Do I clearly see the destruction that my using caused?

Higher Power, help me today to accept
my addiction and to stop using excuses
to avoid the task of recovery.

*One thing I will do today to begin repairing
the damage caused by my using is*

God help me to stay clean and sober today!

APRIL 23

Overcoming the urge

When you feel the urge to use, think it all the way through. This is a critical step in staying away from that first drink, pill, or fix. Sometimes we're confronted with situations where it seems we have no defense against the first one. So then we ask ourselves, *What did my fellow addicts say to do?*

They said; "Think it through" to its logical conclusion. For us that first drink, pill, or fix can mean wreckage and despair. And with such a thought to the consequences, we will gain the resolve to overcome the urge.

Do I know how to overcome the urge?

Higher Power, when my defenses are down, grant me the presence of mind to think the act of using all the way through.

If I feel the urge to use today, I will reflect on the consequences, such as

God help me to stay clean and sober today!

APRIL 24

Dealing with daily problems

For many of us, chemicals were an escape from the trials of the world. We deeply resented them and earnestly sought escape. Simply getting clean and sober did not wipe away all our problems. Now, however, we have an opportunity to deal with them constructively.

If we do not take that first pill, drink, or fix, our problems can be solved, and stumbling blocks can become stepping stones to a better life.

Am I learning how to deal with daily problems?

Higher Power, I pray to accept my
daily problems and for your
help in dealing with them.

*One thing I will do today
to deal constructively with my problems is*

God help me to stay clean and sober today!

Coming alive to life

How important is awareness! By drinking or drugging we tried to dull our awareness, although perhaps we excused some drugs by insisting that we were heightening our awareness. We always wound up with awareness of little but pain. We were deadened and uninterested in life.

Communication is based on awareness: Through communication, we make others aware of us and we are made aware of those around us. Without communication with God, there is no awareness of God working in our lives. If we want to come alive to life, we can begin by paying attention to our Higher Power.

Am I coming alive and paying attention?

I pray to become more aware of my Higher Power and of life.

Today I will slow down and pay closer attention to

God help me to stay clean and sober today!

Doing what it takes

This universe is beautiful, but it doesn't owe us a living. We can't ask for results before we put forth the effort. We can't be using mood-altering drugs and tell ourselves we'll straighten up when we get a job. It doesn't work that way.

We have to be willing to do what it takes to straighten up first—then we get the benefits. We have to be willing to do it God's way, not ours.

Am I willing to do what it takes?

Higher Power, grant me the willingness
to put forth the effort today,
to work the Steps,
to stay sober and clean.

To stay clean and sober today, I will

God help me to stay clean and sober today!

Developing ourselves

We must realize in our hearts that we are becoming better people. We do this by using our highest standards and making our best efforts. We do this, in part, by turning our lives over to God, who will guide us if we sincerely ask.

As we develop, we find we're offering much more to life than just avoiding mood-altering drugs. We are coming to love others and to help them by thinking, feeling, and behaving maturely in all situations.

Am I developing into a better person?

Higher Power, help me realize that my
new life is not just about changing
my past but about developing my
future as well.

Today I will work on developing myself by

God help me to stay clean and sober today!

Practicing humility

Sometimes we puff up our egos and think, *Since I'm overcoming this terrible addiction, I must be very wise.* But it is not through self or our own wisdom that we recover. We recover through the love and guidance of our Higher Power.

If we keep in mind who we are, what we are, and where our hope has come from, we can grow stronger in our recovery. If we forget these basics and rely on our egos, we will grow closer to the streets and to despair.

Am I practicing humility?

I pray to acknowledge my Higher Power
as my source, strength, and hope,
not myself or "intellectual wisdom."

I will practice humility today by

God help me to stay clean and sober today!

APRIL 29

Becoming forgiving

The lack of a forgiving spirit hurts our spiritual progress. Being unforgiving causes resentment, which is always a danger to our new way of life.

We have learned that if we forgive, we will be forgiven; but if we do not forgive, we will not be forgiven. So it seems we are just hurting ourselves by not forgiving others.

Am I forgiving?

Higher Power, help me forgive
each person I need to forgive today.

Today I will forgive

God help me to stay clean and sober today!

Changing our thinking

We have strong ideas. Sometimes, as hard as it is, we need to change our stubborn thinking. We've learned to accept the bad; now we must learn to accept the *good* without falling apart.

Our old reasons for certain actions are no longer valid. It's not that our beliefs and actions have changed; it's just that our reasons have changed.

Is my thinking changing?

Higher Power, help me to simply *accept—*
without having to understand
everything—if waiting
to understand keeps me from
working my program today.

Today I will examine my thinking about

God help me to stay clean and sober today!

MAY 1

Loving ourselves

Our fellowship tells us to take care of ourselves first. It tells us that life and our Twelve Step program come before anyone or anything else. But what if we get too self-centered about this? Taking care of ourselves does not mean being selfish or maliciously hurting others to meet our own needs. What it means is that we learn to love and mature ourselves, because we are important. We are truly closest to ourselves. If we don't love ourselves, who will?

The famous psychologist Erich Fromm says that if people can love productively, then they can also love themselves; if they can love *only* others, then they cannot love at all. This means that, to be able to love others, we need the capacity to love and care for ourselves.

Am I learning to love myself?

Higher Power, help me to love myself so that I may better love you and others.

Today I will work on how I feel about myself by

God help me to stay clean and sober today!

MAY 2

Helping others

We have been given so much help in our addiction through countless other people who have searched for a solution. If others hadn't searched and found, who would have been there to offer us a helping hand? The ones who come after us can help us best by letting us help them.

Newcomers are a constant reminder and source of joy to us. We're on this path together, and we should never forget to be grateful for our fellow addicts.

Do I help others?

Higher Power, help me always to be grateful to the ones who have helped me, and help me offer my hand to others.

Today I will help my fellow addicts by

God help me to stay clean and sober today!

Losing our self-centeredness

The Fourth Step inventory helps us see our character defects. When we take a look at why we resented others, for example, our self-centeredness jumps out at us. In the past we set up situations that helped only ourselves. Then, when things didn't go our way, we quickly became resentful of people (or places or things).

That kind of self-centeredness is what nearly killed us, but we persisted nevertheless. If we use that same persistence in finding and working on our character defects, our self-centeredness will diminish and make way for the growth promised in the Ninth Step prayer.

Am I using my self-centeredness?

> Higher Power, help me find and
> work on my character defects,
> especially my self-centeredness.

Today I will work on my self-centeredness by

God help me to stay clean and sober today!

MAY 4

Expressing love

Now that we've hit bottom and are starting over, clean and sober, we can finally see that without a Higher Power, without love, we are powerless. It's what we've been seeking for ages—and it's been here all along; we just couldn't see it. We need a Higher Power. We need love.

It is the answer to our problems; it can change everything. (But we have so much trouble with it!) We're afraid of love, and we fail to give the love we have to give. Yet every expression of love is sacred, nurturing.

Am I expressing my love?

Higher Power, help me to see my best self, to express it, and to see the best in others.

I will express the love within me today by

God help me to stay clean and sober today!

MAY 5

Acknowledging addiction's power

We talk about mood-altering chemicals as cunning, baffling, and powerful. And it's true—there are many subtle, sly ways in which we set ourselves up to use again. For example, if we preferred one drug, we might try to convince ourselves that it was okay to use a different one. Or, we might say, "Well, I just didn't know it was so dangerous." Some of us just keep hanging around our using "friends."

We may use many tricky, deceitful plans on ourselves in order to go back to using, even though we know these behaviors are dangerous. Even though we know that by setting ourselves up time and again we will only succeed in destroying our program.

Have I stopped setting myself up?

> Higher Power, look out for me
> when I'm not capable of doing so.

> *Today I will remind myself
> of addiction's power by*

God help me to stay clean and sober today!

Being humble

We are always simply servants of our groups, not presidents or authorities. We *all* take turns doing God's work. If we take on more than we can handle, chances are we'll feel martyred or we'll simply drop out. But this is not common when we share ourselves in the true spirit of service.

If we act in the true spirit of humility, cleaning up or putting up chairs will never be too low a task for us, and being a committee member will never be too exalted.

Am I developing humility?

Higher Power, help me to see how I might serve my group today in whatever capacity.

*Today I will practice humility
in serving my brothers and sisters by*

God *help me to stay clean and sober today!*

MAY 7

Returning to sanity

For most of us, staying straight was always very difficult and very serious. Some of us took longer to realize this. The highlight of our insanity was trying to prove that somehow we were different, somehow we could get out of the work that was required, somehow we could find an easier, softer way out than the Twelve Step program.

All this trial and error with our lives on the line. Our "insanity" is extreme at times and nothing short of a spiritual awakening. Guidance from our Higher Power can restore us to sanity.

Is my insanity behind me?

Higher Power, help me learn
how to return to sanity.
Teach me to live in a drug-free world.

I will work my program today by

God help me to stay clean and sober today!

MAY 8

Sticking to the basics

If we don't stick to the basics, we'll lose sight of who we are and where we came from. We are not perfect, spiritual giants. We're drunks, junkies, and pill heads who have found a solution to our living problem, a practical solution to an impractical lifestyle.

And if we forget the basics—where we come from, working the Steps, and attending meetings—we may be subject to unrealistic ideals and illusions. These can get in the way of recovery.

Do I keep it simple?

Higher Power, help me to
keep it simple and stick to the basics.

Today I'll be sure to stick to the basics by

God help me to stay clean and sober today!

Knowing our limitations

If someone asks us for spiritual information or guidance, we must be sure we have spiritual information or guidance before trying to give it away. It's an error to assume that just because we are clean and sober anything we suggest will be correct. There is no shame in saying, "I don't know," or suggesting another source of help. In fact, it's a sign of humility.

It takes great courage to recognize and admit our limitations. When we ask for guidance in helping others, we might listen for that "still small voice within" to tell us whether to move forward or hold back.

Am I learning my limitations?

Higher Power, help me to be of real service to you and your children.

Today I will seek spiritual guidance in helping others by

God help me to stay clean and sober today!

Relating to our Higher Power

The relation of our souls to God is so pure that it is vain to think that we can separate it from any of our being. God speaks to all of our life. There isn't one part that belongs to our Higher Power and other parts that belong to a job, family, friends, interests, and so on.

Our relationship with our Higher Power is sacred, and so all of our life is sacred. God loves beyond all things. God's love and purity enter into all our life. We need but recognize and live by this.

How do I relate to God?

> Higher Power, I know that you see me,
> hear me, and know all my thoughts
> and desires, even the innermost
> secrets of my heart!

Today I will work on my relationship
with my Higher Power by

God help me to stay clean and sober today!

MAY 11

Overcoming indecision

We often find it difficult to make simple decisions in our everyday lives. Sometimes the major decisions are easier to make than minor ones. But it is good practice to ask for help on any issue we need help with, major or minor, simple or complex.

Over time our Higher Power will help us see life situations with increasing clarity. Over time everyday decisions will become easier to make and everyday irritations will stop paralyzing our thinking.

Am I conquering my indecision?

Higher Power, I pray for greater
self-awareness and the willingness
to ask for help with everyday indecision.

Today I will ask for help with

God help me to stay clean and sober today!

MAY 12

Measuring our success

Success and happiness in working our program are subjective. They have to be. Personal satisfaction in anything depends on the individual's perceptions. Members may comment on what makes for success and happiness in the program, but we can only measure it for ourselves. To judge success by another's standards is being untrue to ourselves.

Some judge success in material terms, some in physical terms. Still others judge success in terms of emotional adjustment or mental and spiritual growth. It's up to us and our Higher Power, not family, friends, or therapists. We alone measure our success.

How do I measure *my* success?

Higher Power, grant that all my thoughts,
words, actions, and successes
today will be directed by you.

*Today I will examine my standards
for success and happiness by*

God help me to stay clean and sober today!

Being a friend

If we want to be miserable, let's just think about ourselves. "I'm not getting what I want. That person doesn't treat me right. I don't deserve misfortune." It's easy to be miserable. But if we want happiness, we need to be a friend to someone.

Let's all share our experience, strength, and hope. If we want to know God's love, let us show love. If we want contentment and joy, let us walk and talk with God.

Do I bring happiness to others?

> Higher Power, help me to
> show the love I have.

Today I will be a friend to

God help me to stay clean and sober today!

MAY 14

Staying clean and sober

We know that any skill deteriorates without practice. Likewise, staying drug-free is a skill we develop through practice. We need to learn what skills we have in working our program.

How do we keep ourselves drug-free? Do we pray? Do we take daily inventory? Do we admit when we're wrong? Do we work with others? Do we practice the Steps daily? If we're not doing these things, we're getting self-satisfied, and being too self-satisfied can weaken our skills. If we lose our skills, we may soon lose our sobriety and cleanness.

Am I working on my recovery skills?

Higher Power, help me develop the skills I need to stay clean and sober today.

Today I will not rest on my laurels; I will work my program again by

God help me to stay clean and sober today!

Giving it away each day

Talent, heroism, and personal beauty. Although society admires such qualities, they don't count much when it comes to our all-important Twelfth Step work. This work draws on all our talents and powers, but in ways that are subtle, warm, and personal.

With the help of our Higher Power, we develop the power to soothe, suggest, endure, and love. The Step Twelve encounters that happen every day are more important than the work of the statesman or hero. Our program exists and grows through the giving of Step Twelve.

Do I give it away each day?

Higher Power, help me to see
the joy of being loving and self-sacrificing.

Today I will practice giving by

God help me to stay clean and sober today!

MAY 16

Accepting our condition

It is important to realize that we *are* alcoholics and drug addicts and not *ex*-alcoholics or *ex*-addicts. We accept the fact that we have a chronic illness and that no amount of "discipline" and no magic cure will change that.

We are deluding ourselves if we think we can handle "just a little." If we say, "I *used to be* an alcoholic" or "I *used to be* a drug addict," then we may conclude that we can drink or take drugs and still stay in control. But for us, that's the route to despair and, perhaps, death.

Do I accept my incurable illness?

Higher Power, help me never to forget
who I am, what I am,
and where my salvation lies.

I will practice acceptance today by

God help me to stay clean and sober today!

Overreacting

Those of us with chemical dependency have often shown just how damaging it can be to get too hungry, angry, lonely, or tired. Ironically, what we tend to get upset about aren't the essentials.

Perhaps we can learn not to panic over simple misfortune, ungrounded fears, and emotional turmoil. If we can open ourselves up to a Higher Power and a spiritual practice, we can settle down. We'll feel a lot better about ourselves and the world.

Have I stopped overreacting?

May I welcome a Higher Power
to help me keep perspective and stay calm.

*Today I will deal constructively
with negative emotions by*

God help me to stay clean and sober today!

Handling stress

Sometimes we feel stress—anxious, irritable, achy. We can't think straight. We worry and wonder what's wrong. Before the mountains arose, there was stress in the earth, internal pressure; something had to change. So, too, with us. Before change happens in us, we feel stress. But if we continue to work the Steps, work with others, and attend meetings, one day we will find that we have changed for the better.

Am I learning to handle stress?

> Higher Power, help me keep in mind
> what I want to become; help me stay
> faithful during times of stress.

I will change the way I handle stress today by

God help me to stay clean and sober today!

Living according to principles

If we live according to spiritual principles, we will know harmony in our lives. If we ignore these principles, our harmony will be destroyed.

Fortunately the principles are constant. Once we recognize our mistakes, our task is to once again apply the principles we learned and harmony will return.

Am I living according to spiritual principles?

> Higher Power, help me to be aware of
> and live according to principles.

Today I will apply my spiritual principles by

God help me to stay clean and sober today!

MAY 20

Looking for a Higher Power

To stay clean of mood-altering chemicals, it is important to find a Higher Power—a *personal* Higher Power. Not one based on someone else's ideas, not one based on someone else's beliefs, but a Higher Power that speaks intimately to us alone.

Our histories are different; our recoveries are different. The kind of relationship we develop with our Higher Power may well be different too.

Am I finding my personal Higher Power?

I pray to develop a *personal* relationship with my Higher Power.

Today I will work in a personal relationship with my Higher Power by

God help me to stay clean and sober today!

MAY 21

Passing it on

Before we can help others, we must first help ourselves. If we acknowledge our chemical dependency problems and seek to change, we are growing. In growing, we have something to offer others.

As those before us have helped us grow, we in turn, can help others grow. We can pass it on.

Am I growing and passing it on?

Higher Power, help me realize that as I grow through your love, others grow through my love for them.

Today I will share my love and growth with

God help me to stay clean and sober today!

MAY 22

Accepting tragedy

Even clean and sober, there may be tragic experiences in our lives. Sometimes there is just no logical explanation. Unexplained misery seems cruel, and we wonder how God can do this to God's children. We don't know the answers.

We know that many of our problems are of our own making. But what do we do about acts of God? It is said that our greatest burdens may also be our greatest gifts and that the most tragic experience can help us learn to be of service and at one with our Creator.

Am I capable of accepting tragedy?

I can't, my Higher Power can—and will—
if I allow it.

I will practice acceptance today by

God help me to stay clean and sober today!

Listening

A common saying in the program is "If you don't like what you hear at this meeting, leave it here." Many people do just that, they leave *everything* at the meetings. Most of us did not get better by listening only to what we wanted to hear.

What helped us in the long run was listening to things we didn't want to hear, such as "Work the Steps, you're no better than anyone else," and "Don't take that first fix, pill, or drink." The hard work of recovery, the things we don't want to do, are often the very things that make it possible for us to arrest our disease.

Am I listening to what I need to hear?

Higher Power, grant me the courage
to listen to the hard things and apply
them in my program today.

Today I will listen to

God help me to stay clean and sober today!

Accepting our addiction

I can't be a drug addict or an alcoholic because I can quit anytime I want to, because I use only on weekends, because I never drink anything but beer or use anything but grass, because I am too young. We have heard these excuses many times and perhaps we have used them ourselves. But ignorance and denial can kill us.

Only honest acceptance of the truth can free us from our addiction. Old-timers are fond of saying that people don't get to this program by mistake. If we are reading this page today, let's hope all these excuses are behind us.

Have I stopped denying my addiction?

God, grant me the courage to let go of the excuses and accept the truth about myself.

I will acknowledge my addiction today by

God help me to stay clean and sober today!

MAY 25

Living in the now

"Just for today." "Live in the now." "It's a twenty-four-hour program." Ask for sobriety and cleanness each day upon arising. Take a daily inventory.

Such slogans and recommendations show that our predecessors considered the twenty-four-hour approach to be pretty important.

Can I see how this is true? Do I practice living one day at a time?

God, grant me the patience to live in today and the insight for a better tomorrow.

Today I will work at living in the now by

God help me to stay clean and sober today!

Hanging-on days

Some days in this program you just have to "hang on." Somehow we lose contact with our Higher Power and we don't feel right about anything. So we need to learn what to do to get reconnected, what to do to feel better.

Pray. Meditate. Keep in touch with fellow addicts and our sponsor. Work the Steps. Hang on. Time will take away most of our fears, but we should expect, and be prepared for, some days of just "hanging on." The important point is: Do I have something to hang on to?

> Higher Power, on those days
> when I am just hanging on,
> let me hang on to your love for me.

I will strengthen my hold on sobriety today by

God help me to stay clean and sober today!

Waiting for answers

We are full of questions and we want answers, answers that just aren't available to us yet. Our Higher Power will give us the real answers when we can handle them, not before. If we manufacture our own answers, our self-will will only create more questions.

Wishes and answers are granted and guided by our Higher Power—provided we keep close enough to be ready for them.

Am I willing to wait for the true answers?

Higher Power, help me to accept my questions and to wait for the true answers.

Today I will prepare myself for answers to my problems by

God help me to stay clean and sober today!

Being honest

After we've been in the program for a while, we may not be as honest with ourselves as we were at first. It's not easy to stay vigilant. Keep taking our inventory, and look for defects that may have cropped up.

It helps to ask our Higher Power for insight so we can see all our defects. We need honesty to stay clean and sober.

Am I staying honest with myself?

Higher Power, help me to fear my faults less; help me to be honest with myself.

*I will work on being
honest with myself today by*

God help me to stay clean and sober today!

MAY 29

Sharing in the fellowship

It is said that you can always tell a roomful of recovering addicts because everyone is smoking, drinking coffee, and talking—all at the same time. There is serious truth to this wry glance at the fellowship.

Since the program, its slogans are talked about at length. It's easy for anyone to learn a lot about recovery. Since people's everyday problems are talked about all the time, it's enough for anyone to learn about life. It all works! Our big mouths—mouths that kept us sick for so long—are now flapping to keep us well.

So our sometimes smoke-filled, coffee-filled, talk-filled clubs, meetings, and social gatherings are the basis for a lot more than laughter—they add up to a major part of our recovery.

Am I contributing to the fellowship?

Higher Power, help me see
what I can contribute to the
social life fellowship of recovery.

Today I will take part in the fellowship by

God help me to stay clean and sober today!

MAY 30

Paying attention

Planning our own speech during a discussion meeting makes it hard to listen. Recovery requires silence and attention.

Sometime, somewhere, something we've heard in a meeting may come to mind just when we need it. But if we sit at meetings engrossed in our own thoughts, we can't learn the suggestions we may need to help us in times of danger.

Do I pay close attention at meetings?

Higher Power, help me to
open my ears and close my mouth
just a little more today.

I will practice staying focused today by

God help me to stay clean and sober today!

Living today well

Our Higher Power's will for us is always better than our own, but we cannot see this truth unless we let go enough to venture into the new areas to which we are being led. To experience growth, we must let go of old ideas. (Our old ideas fit only our drug world.)

Each day, well lived, moves us closer to what we are seeking. We must become more giving and more willing to use what we have today.

Am I living today well?

> Higher Power,
> help me accept your will
> for me today.

I will live today well by

God help me to stay clean and sober today!

JUNE 1

Practicing virtue

Love, justice, honesty, and patience are virtues, are ways to God. But even virtues can become defects if we misuse them. Love misused turns into possessiveness, justice into cold facts, honesty into brutal frankness, patience into irritable silence.

We need to know ourselves to understand what we're doing and where we're going. We need to look at ourselves to make sure that we have not misused our virtues and made them destructive. We must make sure we do not become self-righteous.

Do I practice virtue constructively?

Higher Power, help me not be so eager that my virtues turn into defects.

I will practice virtue humbly today by

God help me to stay clean and sober today!

JUNE 2

Understanding

Absolute statements are almost always wrong: All blacks are *this*; all whites are *that*; all men are *this*; all women are *that*; all addicts are (whatever). But here's a statement that holds up under examination: We are all stumbling human beings.

Therefore, we all need to become as understanding as we can, for without understanding, we do not grant others their right to be "human."

Do I overlook the shortcomings of others?

Higher Power, help me keep in mind
that every woman is my sister
and every man my brother.

I will be more accepting of my fellows today by

God help me to stay clean and sober today!

JUNE 3

Accepting ourselves

Many of us used to think that our Higher Power hates this or that about us or about others, but our Higher Power doesn't hate at all. Our Higher Power accepts us and loves us no matter how we have lived. It understands that we are capable of changing.

This is the only way we come to know God, even as we begin to accept ourselves and others. The ability to accept ourselves more and more is a gift from God. It comes as we build upon the strong, valuable parts of ourselves.

Am I learning to accept myself?

Higher Power, help me believe in your acceptance, forgiveness, and generosity; help me to be willing to see myself in a new way.

Today I will work on self-acceptance by

God help me to stay clean and sober today!

Telling tales

We have such egos. Even when we talk about our troubled past, it often sounds as though we're bragging. We seem to take pride in how we used drugs, how much and how often we used them. We build up our stories and often try to top the other guy's drug-alogue. It seems we're saying, "See how good I am! I don't do those things anymore."

But now that we're in recovery, now that we have a choice in our behavior, trying to impress others with our past doesn't show serene, spiritual people—it shows insecure, egocentric braggarts.

Am I a storyteller?

> Lord, help me avoid glorifying
> my story to impress myself and others.

To keep my story straight today I will

God help me to stay clean and sober today!

JUNE 5

Taking the Fourth Step

It is very easy, when talking in general terms, to sweep away our past and say we want forgiveness and understanding of our wrongs. But this should not be confused with doing a Fourth Step. There, we don't generalize or simplify the nature of our wrongs; we talk about their exact nature. If we put this on a personal level, we begin to see how difficult the inventory Steps are.

Often we must pray for the willingness to go on. Becoming willing to be specific may be the hardest thing we've ever had to do. But seeing the living miracles around us testifies to the fact that the rewards are great. If we are willing, God provides the opportunities for working the Steps.

Have I stopped generalizing about my defects?

Higher Power, help me be specific about the exact nature of my wrongs.

Today I will be specific about my defects, including

God help me to stay clean and sober today!

JUNE 6

Avoiding self-pity

Our troubled lives and mixed-up emotions can easily draw pity from those who would help us. Sometimes we even exaggerate our history or current situation to get more pity. In the program we share our feelings to avoid self-pity because we know how destructive it can be.

When we say, "This too shall pass," for example, we are not giving our fellows the brush-off. Rather we are saying, "Don't wallow in self-pity; it's a killer. We've all experienced similar situations. God loves you and it *will* pass!"

Have I stopped pitying myself?

Higher Power, help me to remember
that pity leads only to self-pity
and that I want to change that pattern.

Today I will work on avoiding self-pity by

God help me to stay clean and sober today!

Awaken spiritually

Many of us have had spiritual experiences and spiritual awakenings as a result of this program. Some people had them before they arrived, some when they first arrived, some years after. But before we come to realize a power greater than ourselves or our addiction, we don't need to hear voices or see visions.

The spiritual experience most of us have is a quiet realization that God has given us our lives. What greater experience can we ask for?

Have I had a spiritual awakening?

Higher Power, help me remain grateful for the gift of my life.

I will practice my spiritual aliveness today by

God help me to stay clean and sober today!

Helping slippers

Why do they have to suffer? Why is it that we have found and accepted this fellowship while some people seem unable to or else must experience untold hardships before they can accept it? Many times our hearts have ached at the seeming failure of Twelfth Step work.

We watch others suffer needlessly and sometimes die. We watch others repeatedly slip and our hearts cry out to them. Those of us who make it must never give up on the ones who don't. They need us desperately and we need them. Even if they truly can't make it, God still loves them all.

Do I leave the results of my Twelfth Step work with my Higher Power?

All God's children are in God's hands. Thank you for the way you are holding me!

Today I will try to help a person who has slipped by

God help me to stay clean and sober today!

JUNE 9

Living miracles

When people abuse alcohol and other drugs month after month, it seems that only a miracle can take them out of their depths of despair. But the miracle is not having a great vision or experience. Rather we need only do our daily task.

If we practice patience, faith, and love amidst the turmoil of the day, we will have great opportunity for a clean, joyful life. If we practice the needs of the spirit, we will become our own living miracles.

Am I living spiritually?

> Higher Power, may I act more in
> your spirit in my daily activities.

I will practice living spiritually today by

God help me to stay clean and sober today!

JUNE 10

Being foolish

Many of us could say that what we have gained from this program we've gained in spite of ourselves. We get in our own way and often block ourselves from our Higher Power and fellow addicts. In the beginning, we did foolish things such as going to places where drugs or alcohol are used, deliberately setting ourselves up to take that first drink or drug.

Even when we make such mistakes, God still accepts us. We can still choose to pray and ask for help. Even with our foolish moments, in spite of ourselves, God will help if we ask.

Am I becoming less foolish these days?

Higher Power, help me become
more aware of my own foolish thoughts,
and help me avoid acting on them.

Today I will try to stay out of my own way by

God help me to stay clean and sober today!

JUNE 11

Being an addict

Sometimes people feel more qualified to be members of the program because they feel they have suffered more physical deprivation. But this does not really matter: An addict is an addict, pain is pain, suffering is suffering.

You can be an addict and suffer whether you have holes in your pants or a new suit, an empty belly or a full one.

Do I realize that addiction and suffering are a state of mind?

Higher Power, help me see that pain is pain and that I cannot judge it for anyone.

Today I will help those who still suffer, whether rich or poor, by

God help me to stay clean and sober today!

JUNE 12

Letting go of our defects

We're not like everyone else. We demand attention. We would die if we found out we're not the center of a few lives. We want reassurances that we're coming across as the generous, honorable people we are striving to become, but we soon realize that character defects and self-centeredness still plague us.

When we get a glimpse from time to time of how others see us, it can be a dreadful, painful experience. If it weren't for the loving attitude of our fellow addicts, many of us could not endure it. But the growth process is worth the pain as we find out that we're gradually becoming the generous, honorable people that we want to be.

Am I letting go of my defects?

Higher Power, help me to see myself
as I truly am to begin to let go of
my character defects.

Today I will work on self-centeredness by

God help me to stay clean and sober today!

JUNE 13

Doing our best

Doing our best takes more time and energy, but the rewards are great. In staying clean and sober, it may mean feeling in tune, feeling committed, feeling successful—in short, serenity.

For many of us the fear of failure keeps us from putting everything we have into living. And when we don't succeed, we always have the ready excuse, "I wasn't really trying." But the more we give to anything, the more we *have* to give, and the better we feel about ourselves.

Do I always put forth my best effort?

Higher Power, help me to accept
my fear and do my best.

*I will do my best today—
even if I feel afraid—to*

God help me to stay clean and sober today!

JUNE 14

Going to meetings

Many of us have many problems: financial, legal, and emotional. If we asked fellow members for advice, they might well say, "Go to a meeting." Going to meetings is not just something we do in our spare time. Meetings are a way to find answers, get support, and generally maintain our recovery.

What kind of advice is that—"go to a meeting"—for practical problems? But it works! For other people, this would not work; but for those of us in recovery from chemical dependency, it is the beginning of solutions to our problems. Meetings are not "spare time"; they're critical "life time."

Am I making the most out of meetings?

God, help me develop faith in the fellowship and deep respect for meetings.

*Today I will make plans
to attend the meeting at*

God help me to stay clean and sober today!

JUNE 15

Being different

Some of us feel so different that we think no person or group could help us or even understand us. We feel alone and isolated. Whatever these differences are they can be lessened by concentrating on the purpose common to us all: we are learning to live a life free of alcohol or other drugs by connecting with a power greater than ourselves.

Our Higher Power does not want us to be alone. It would help if we would accept that we are all more alike than different. It would help if we could recognize the love that is available to us in our brothers and sisters. Are we looking for what we have in common, or are we looking for ways to be alone and different?

Do I realize that our common purpose can outweigh all differences?

Higher Power, help me feel connected by looking for what I share with my fellow members.

Today I will overlook all differences or look for what we share in

God help me to stay clean and sober today!

JUNE 16

Taking off the masks

We're not much different from other people (except that we couldn't stop abusing mood-altering chemicals). Like other people, we, too, wear masks. We're afraid that others will find out who we really are, especially since we no longer hide behind chemicals.

But if we work the program, we will get stronger. If we work the program, we won't need our masks because we will accept ourselves (and others) more.

Can I stop wearing my masks?

Higher Power, help me work the Steps and to accept myself and my recovery.

Today I will practice treating myself well. I will practice being myself with

God help me to stay clean and sober today!

Growing stronger

We are just one drink, pill, or fix away from relapse. But each day of abstinence makes us stronger. And over time, as we strive for spiritual progress, we become familiar with our resistances and our strengths.

Ralph Waldo Emerson wrote that "this kind of person increases his skill and strength and learns the favorable moments and the favorable accidents. He is his own apprentice, and more time gives a great addition of power, just as a falling body acquires momentum with every foot of the fall."

Is my recovery growing steadier and stronger?

Higher Power, may my striving for spiritual growth bring self-understanding and strength to my recovery.

I will strengthen my recovery today by

God help me to stay clean and sober today!

Letting go of self-will

Self-will is what brought us to our knees. We must realize now that we can either make our will one with our Higher Power or we can remain separate. When we exercise un-controlled self-will, things crumble before us and often we find ourselves in the streets again. But this need not happen because now we know the difference; we have a choice.

When we let go and make our will one with our Higher Power's, we have no trouble avoiding mood-altering chemicals.

Have I turned my will over?

I pray that I might let my will become one with my Higher Power.

Today I will let go of my self-will by

God help me to stay clean and sober today!

JUNE 19

Doing the footwork

We often ask our Higher Power for spiritual assets without recognizing the work we need to do to get them. To grow strong, we must learn to carry burdens; to gain patience, we must learn to handle stress; to follow God's will, we must become willing to let go. To be courageous, we must practice faith in the face of fear; to be right, we must learn to admit wrongs; to be loved, we must learn to be loving.

Our Higher Power gives us opportunities to grow. The footwork is up to us.

Am I doing my part?

Higher Power, help me to recognize, and do, my part in recovery.

Today I will do the footwork necessary to

God help me to stay clean and sober today!

JUNE 20

Looking for beauty

It is important that we look for beauty. There are beautiful things in the world each and every day, if we only know how to see.

In recovery, in serenity, beauty is everywhere—even in pain and suffering—if we only know how to see.

How good am I at seeing all the beauty there is to see?

Higher Power, help me to use my recovery, my new vision, to see beauty.

Today I will practice looking for beauty in

God help me to stay clean and sober today!

Dealing with problems

Eventually we reach a point in recovery where one trying incident doesn't have to ruin the whole day. We reach a point where we're less sensitive or emotional. We learn to take each day with everything in it. We learn to take each day with humor, acceptance, and love.

This is not to say that we become doormats; it just means we're going to find ways to calm down and not complicate existing problems. Just for today, let's leave all our trials and complications to our Higher Power.

Am I learning to be less sensitive or emotional?

> Higher Power, when I start to feel
> the pressure of today's tribulations,
> help me remember that you can
> handle anything.

My plan for handling problems today is

God help me to stay clean and sober today!

Overcoming loneliness

Chances are, we considered ourselves loners when we came into the program. Some of us had divided the world into the people who hated us and the people who didn't like us very much. Some of us felt very alone even though we knew people liked us.

We never have to be alone again, however. By staying sober and clean, the walls we built around ourselves gradually come down.

Have I stopped being a loner?

Lord, help me to do what I need to do
to never be alone again.

I will avoid loneliness today by

God help me to stay clean and sober today!

Becoming patient

Let us not rush and demand perfection all at once; it would only blind us. If we are impatient, it is impossible to work a daily program; but if we are patient, we can learn to see our daily opportunities for growth.

We can't develop a new relationship with our Higher Power overnight. It is worth waiting for, striving for. Let us not go too fast but simply count each day as an opportunity.

Am I learning patience?

Higher Power, I pray that I may be patient
as I work my program and
develop a relationship with you.

Today I will practice patience with

God help me to stay clean and sober today!

Getting honest

There is an intuitive understanding between recovering addicts and newcomers. Old-timers know well the games that newcomers play at first. Newcomers are not asked what they're thinking, they're told what they're thinking! They don't need to be trapped into lies; old-timers tell them the lies they were about to tell.

Thus, in the beginning, we start to get honest because we hardly have a choice. We give up on playing games because there are no tricks left in the bag. Being confronted by others, we *have* to get honest—honest enough to save our lives.

Have I stopped playing games? Am I getting more honest?

Higher Power, let me be grateful for the intuition and quick tongue of my fellow members: They can help me get honest.

I will practice honesty today by

God help me to stay clean and sober today!

JUNE 25

Analyzing

Our constant analyzing could mean we don't work the Steps; eventually, it could cost us our lives. It's as if we were standing in a burning building, in front of a fire escape, trying to understand the principles of oxidation.

What we need to do first is to *get out of the fire;* we can learn about oxidation—about addiction and recovery—later. It is dangerous to stand on the fringes of addiction; it can be dangerous to delay a commitment.

Have I made a clear choice?

Higher Power, help me learn to relate to you as well as to my analytical mind.

Today I will let go of analyzing and take Steps

God help me to stay clean and sober today!

Listening by reading

We need to listen to drug-free members of the program to hear what it takes to stay clean and sober. But "listening" is not limited to meetings: There is a lot of literature that discusses the program and how to work it more effectively.

When we first come into the program, it is wise to keep our mouths shut and our eyes and ears open. Reading books, magazines, and pamphlets is an important way of listening. It is a gift from our fellow addicts that so much listening is available to us.

Am I well read on the program?

Higher Power, help me to "listen"
in all the ways available to me.

Today I will read

God help me to stay clean and sober today!

Dropping biases

Addiction is not biased, nor should we be biased in the program. Whatever our beliefs before we found this solution, it helps if we avoid letting them interfere with our Step Twelve work. There are few enough places where people are accepted regardless of status, religion, nationality, or appearance.

Each of us needs everyone else in the fellowship. Whether laborer or judge, white or black, addict or alcoholic, if she or he can carry the message of recovery, he or she can save your life. Am I letting go of all bias?

Higher Power, help me let go of my biases
so that I can better help save lives.

*Today I will take an inventory of my biases
and practice letting them go by*

God help me to stay clean and sober today!

Practicing

To recover, we must change; it doesn't happen by itself. Change requires practice. If we get lazy about our recovery, if we get smug or self-satisfied, we may stop practicing. If so, we may lose what we have gained, risk a slip, or even relapse.

In recovery, practice is all-important. Staying clean and sober takes practice. For starters, we must practice carrying the message to others who still suffer.

Higher Power, help me practice
the program so that I can keep growing
and recovering.

Today I will work on

God help me to stay clean and sober today!

JUNE 29

Living the "today" approach

We must understand from the very beginning that in the program, we learn to live one day at a time. We learn, for example, not to take that first fix, pill, or drink "today." This is easier for us to do than to think of abstaining for years or a lifetime.

But many of us miss the fact that the "today" approach can be applied to all areas of our life, not just abstinence. It helps if we can deal with issues such as love, sex, death, honesty, and resentments one day at a time. God expects no more of us than to do what we can do today.

Am I living "today" today?

God, help me live the "today" approach in all areas of my life.

Today I will apply the "today" approach to

God help me to stay clean and sober today!

JUNE 30

Being clean and sober

Being clean and sober means much more than just being abstinent; it's a state of mind. Simply staying away from that first fix, pill, or drink is not the only goal. If we are merely abstinent and are not actively working on our recovery, we will still crave alcohol or other drugs.

Being in recovery means not just abstinence but a way of life. In recovery we try to become better people and in the process, find we no longer *need* a fix, pill, or drink. This is the difference between abstinence and being in recovery.

Am I actively working on my recovery?

Higher Power, I am grateful
for my abstinence, and I pray for your help
to do what I need to do to recover.

I will work on my recovery today by

God help me to stay clean and sober today!

JULY 1

Seeking freedom

If we want freedom from addiction, we must start the process ourselves. Then we must accept any help offered and follow the direction of our Higher Power. Recovery does not come to us without effort. First we seek abstinence; we want to be clean and sober. Later, we look for the joys of living.

It often takes months and years to grasp the principles that will set us free. But free of what? At first, freedom from alcohol and other drugs; then, freedom from fear and from anything else that binds us. To become free, we can begin seeking our principles and our truth today.

Am I seeking freedom?

Higher Power, help me become
free from the things that bind me.

Today I will work toward freedom from

God help me to stay clean and sober today!

JULY 2

Overcoming worry ←

Worrying only succeeds in ruining our days and driving us nuts. It's better if we don't burden ourselves with what we need to do until we need to do it—and then promptly do it. And if worry weakens, action strengthens. If we stay active, we don't have time to worry.

Our Higher Power knows our needs and will give us the knowledge and power to get them if we wholly trust. Besides, why worry when we can pray?

Do I let God help me with my worries?

Higher Power, help me to stay active
and to trust that you'll take care of me.

I will practice not worrying today by

God help me to stay clean and sober today!

JULY 3

Sharing our program

Sharing is truly valuable. It doesn't simply help the other guy; it helps us too. By sharing how our program is working, we get the feedback we need (positive or negative) to see clearly. It helps us to see regularly how we are doing.

We can spare ourselves unnecessary pain if we take our experiences to meetings for feedback. As we develop our lives, it helps to know what others are doing to develop theirs.

Am I sharing my problems and progress with others?

Higher Power, help me truly share
my recovery so that I can help myself
and others.

Today I will share my program with

God help me to stay clean and sober today!

JULY 4

Staying clean and sober through the holidays

Holidays have been the time when getting high was easiest to justify. Either we joined in the festivities, or we used our sadness, anxiety, or anger as an excuse. Now that we are clean and sober, we realize that on holidays we don't *have to* escape anymore. We have a choice.

We wake up in the morning, appreciate being clean and sober, and just live the day to the best of our abilities. No longer do we fear the festivities, the free time or pressures; no longer do we fear our sadness, anxiety, or anger.

Am I overcoming the need to escape?

Thank you, Higher Power,
for this day (as well as all others);
may I make the most of it.

I will make the most of today's holiday by

God help me to stay clean and sober today!

JULY 5

Praying

Our prayers are always answered, but sometimes the answer is no and sometimes the answer is one we cannot understand. (How can we understand the plans of our Higher Power?) If we trust our Higher Power to keep us clean and sober, perhaps our faith can extend to other areas of our lives.

There is a saying in the program about prayer that makes a lot of sense: We should work every day as if everything depended on us and pray every day as if everything depended on God.

Am I praying with faith?

Higher Power, help me ask for
what I need and to trust what I get.

Today I will pray for

God help me to stay clean and sober today!

JULY 6
First things first

There is no substitute for the Twelve Step program, but that doesn't exclude other forms of mutual or professional help. Some of us may need a firm foundation in the program, however, before other activities and therapies can be added without causing confusion.

If we are chemically dependent, we need to work with others who are chemically dependent in order to recover. If we combine other kinds of help to meet our needs, we neglect our Twelve Step work at the risk of relapse. Am I putting first things first?

Higher Power, help me realize
what my program does for me
and to keep it strong.

*I will make a commitment
to my program today by*

God help me to stay clean and sober today!

JULY 7

Carrying the message

None of us is the ultimate Twelfth-Stepper. Carrying the message of Step Twelve is one of the most important aspects of our recovery, but it can become a problem. The danger is when we try to impress people or get grandiose rather than simply carry the message.

It is not our power or personality that helps people on Step Twelve calls; rather it's the power and truth of the program working through us. It makes our hands steady and clears our minds. We only carry the message; God delivers it.

Am I a good Twelfth-Stepper?

Higher Power, in carrying the message of recovery to those who still suffer, help me be clear and humble.

Today I will practice humility by

God help me to stay clean and sober today!

Letting go of anger

As long as anger dominates us, it is difficult to make progress in the program. Some of the ways anger shows up include gossip, slander, backstabbing, profanity, fault-finding, resentment, quarrelsomeness, impatience, mockery, and irritability. We are all guilty of these behaviors to some degree, probably every day.

Anger is a pattern that we need to change to make progress. It has probably caused more grief than any other character defect. To let go of anger, we inventory it; we pray to release it and to practice not getting angry.

Am I working on my anger?

Higher Power, help me to practice
the virtues of patience and love.
When I am loving, I cannot be angry.

*I will inventory my anger today,
and then I will*

God help me to stay clean and sober today!

Working on problems

Once we're clean and sober, then we complain about all our problems: We have bills, we want a job, we want sex, we want more clothes, and so on. Typically, we are encouraged not to worry about these problems and just work the program! It is hard to believe that they will work themselves out as we work our program, but they do.

Our Higher Power will take care of us as long as we do the necessary footwork. But doing the footwork doesn't include much complaining, it means working the Steps. Our problems will be taken care of as a result of our work.

Can I work more (and complain less)?

Higher Power, as I work the program, help me believe that all your promises to me will be fulfilled.

Instead of staying stuck complaining, today I will work on

God help me to stay clean and sober today!

Avoiding criticism

Criticism is hard to take. If we don't want to be criticized, we shouldn't criticize others. At the same time, expressing concern in a loving way is not being critical.

We are entitled to our opinions, but we are not entitled to put other people down. Sharing our experience, strength, and hope is a way to help others, not to make them feel small.

Can I express loving concern? Can I share without making comparisons?

> Higher Power, help me recognize
> when I am becoming critical;
> help me to be loving and humble.

Today I will praise

God help me to stay clean and sober today!

Showing empathy

When we first got into recovery, most of us were quite unhappy. We were in pain; we were vulnerable. We were angry and impatient. We probably didn't like ourselves very much and may not have liked other people much.

But what if others had treated us according to these feelings? Weren't we forgiven? Accepted? (And if we weren't, wouldn't it have been better if we had been?) Today, we see that we are the same as everyone else who is struggling to achieve or maintain a drug-free life. If we treat everyone well, it will help us recover.

Am I practicing generosity and compassion?

> Higher Power, help me to treat others
> as I would want to be treated.

*Today I will be especially compassionate
toward*

God help me to stay clean and sober today!

JULY 12

Knowing our Higher Power

A good understanding of our Higher Power may be necessary for some of us, but we don't need to get stuck on any image. All we have to do is become willing to believe that a power greater than ourselves will help us get clean and sober.

Electricity works the same *after* a course in electronics as it did *before* the course. Likewise, our Higher Power works the same for us before we understand how it operates. It gets down to this simple idea: It's less important that we understand God than believe God understands us.

Do I have faith in my Higher Power?

Higher Power, help me accept the fact
that understanding your ways
is less important than believing
you are present in my life today.

*I will apply my faith in my
Higher Power today by*

God help me to stay clean and sober today!

Lacking power over others

When we look closely at our lives, we may realize that we have little power over others (as shocking as that may seem). Yet often our arrogance gets so blown out of proportion that we think our actions can get people high or keep them straight! Think of that!

We are so important to ourselves, we begin to think that we are that important to others. We seldom see that our affairs have about as much weight with others as theirs do with us—and that is often little.

Do I realize that I can manage no one?

Higher Power, help me realize that my power over others is actually slight and protect me from my own arrogance.

*If I find myself trying to
manage others today, I will*

God help me to stay clean and sober today!

Paying for freedom

Henry David Thoreau said, "The cost of a thing is the amount of what I will call life which is required to be exchanged for it, immediately or in the long run." The price we paid for using alcohol and other drugs was our freedom. We finally realized that it costs too much to feel oblivious. The price became so high that we could no longer barter with mood-altering chemicals for our time and freedom. The chemicals had absolute control.

Unless we wake up and pay the price for freedom—which is spiritual growth—we will be a slave to chemicals until death. But if we turn our lives over to God, all the liberty we need is made available to us.

Am I paying the right price for my freedom?

Higher Power, help me always to remember that the cost of using chemicals in my life is much too high.

Today I will pay for greater freedom by

God help me to stay clean and sober today!

Recognizing opportunities

Today is a day of opportunity. Any experiences that we have today—good or bad—can be seen as opportunities, opportunities to grow closer to God.

As bread is food for the body, opportunities are food for the soul.

Do I see all the opportunities in my daily life? Do I take advantage of them?

> I pray that I may use my experiences
> as opportunities to grow closer to God.

Today I will look for opportunities by

God help me to stay clean and sober today!

JULY 16

Putting our own recovery first

After we have put together a few months of recovery, we may really want to help others in our meeting. The goal is worthy, but we must be careful that we don't find it easier to worry about others' recovery than our own.

In recovery we all have plenty to do on our own. We need to concentrate on ourselves, especially at first. This is not being selfish; it's putting "first things first." Chances are, we can be more helpful to our brothers and sisters if we simply (although not easily) set a good example, that is, if we go to meetings, work with a sponsor, pray, and do regular inventories.

Am I setting a good example?

> Higher Power, help me simply to do
> my own work and not worry about
> others' work.

Today I will set a good example by

God help me to stay clean and sober today!

Becoming willing to act

The miracles in our program don't simply rub off at meetings. The key to getting clean and sober—and staying clean and sober—is a willingness to act.

Once we feel scared enough or strong enough to do something—once the willingness appears—miracles can happen. *Action* is the magic word. We must not wait for something to "rub off." Rather, we must act as soon as possible. An important phrase in the program describes this: "acting as if."

Am I learning to "act as if"?

Higher Power, help me become willing to act so that I don't fall into a spiritual sleep.

Today I will take action on

God help me to stay clean and sober today!

Practicing sanity

When we were getting high all the time, we were practicing insanity. It was a lot of fun. We got so good at it, however, that we couldn't tell see how serious it had become. Whether we're straight or high, insanity seemed to take over.

Now we can practice sanity daily. Practicing anything will eventually make us pretty good at it. With the grace of God, we can get pretty good at sanity too.

Am I letting go of my insane behavior?

> Higher Power, help me face the
> fears of sane living, fears I
> tried to hide from with addiction.

> *Today I will reflect on my
> unresolved problem behaviors by*

God help me to stay clean and sober today!

Taking just one

It's that first fix, pill, or drink that gets us high. It's not the second or third or fourth one, or the second day or the second week of using that gets us into trouble. *It is the first one.* And until we understand this concept, we will keep trying—without success—to gain control over our drug use.

For us, control no longer exists. And it never will. When we start thinking, *Well, just one won't hurt me*, we are on our way back to that same pain and discouragement of a drug-filled life.

Do I believe that even one is too many?

Higher Power, please help me
remember that I can never
regain control over my drug use.

*I will avoid taking that first drink
or drug today by*

God help me to stay clean and sober today!

Making a decision

We made a decision, a decision to try this program because all else had failed. (We still doubted it would work, but we were desperate.) This decision was made mostly on hope and a belief. At first, it did not reflect belief in a Higher Power but belief in other people.

When we make a decision to do whatever is necessary, our belief can grow. It can grow to a point where no power on earth can shake our foundation. And from this foundation we can, in turn, offer hope to others in need. We can plant in them the same seeds of belief that made it possible for us to be clean and sober.

Is my belief growing?

> Higher Power, help me stay strong
> in the program and help others
> who need to establish roots.

*Today I will renew my commitment
to the program and its members by*

God help me to stay clean and sober today!

Judging other addicts

As addicts, we tend to judge each other in a cruel way; it can help us feel better about ourselves. For example, alcoholics look down on junkies, junkies look down on speed freaks, and everyone looks down on glue-sniffers. But what's the difference?

We're all in this *together*. We're dealing with life-and-death matters. Making value judgments about the kind or severity of another's addiction is a childish and dangerous game.

Have I stopped judging other addicts?

Higher Power, help me accept myself— and accept others—in all aspects of life.

I will acknowledge someone addicted to another chemical today by

God help me to stay clean and sober today!

Being rational

As practicing addicts, we were impulsive. We just did what we felt like doing. We didn't think things through. Actually, we didn't *think* much at all. We often acted irrationally.

As recovering addicts, we may still have some distorted ideas and may still behave irrationally at times. That's okay. But if what we're doing seems serious to our sponsor or a couple of recovering friends, we need to talk more about our actions.

Am I learning to use reason to test my actions?

Higher Power, help me plant both feet
on the ground and to practice
sharing my thoughts.

I will talk with my sponsor today about

God help me to stay clean and sober today!

Baby-sitting

If someone truly wants our help to stop using mood-altering chemicals, we have a responsibility to do all we can. But demanding that someone accept our help or baby-sitting someone who continues to use probably does more harm than good.

Deep down, we know when someone is sincerely seeking help. While it is our job to carry the message, we must avoid trying to fix someone who is not yet ready to quit. It works better if we tell them we're happy to talk anytime they want to call.

Am I learning the boundary between helping and fixing?

Higher Power, help me help others
according to their needs,
in the best way I can.

I will concentrate on helping myself today by

God help me to stay clean and sober today!

JULY 24

Sharing a common goal

Since we're going the same way, let's go together. We may have some differences, but let's work them out and respect each other's opinions. Since our goal is the same, you help me and I'll help you.

But let's never withhold love as a weapon against one another. Since we are held together by a critical common solution, let's not cause one another any suffering.

Am I learning to emphasize our common purpose?

Higher Power, help me see that
what we share in the fellowship
is more important than what separates us.

Today I will strengthen our common cause by

God help me to stay clean and sober today!

Practicing the principles

Our program and its principles apply to every area of our lives. Sometimes people say that they would lose their livelihood if they applied the principles to their work. But this is probably not true and speaks of fear. If we must lie or be hypocritical in *any* area of our lives, then we are not applying the principles.

Once we realize that it is reassuring and rewarding—not threatening—to let God work through us all the time, we will feel genuine, we will feel integrity, we will feel at peace.

Do I practice these principles in *all* my affairs?

> Higher Power, help me see whether
> any area of my life is missing the
> benefit of the principles.

*The principle I will apply today
in all my affairs is*

God help me to stay clean and sober today!

JULY 26

Avoiding pity

Coming into the fellowship, newcomers may see older members as unsympathetic, unsupportive, or even rude. Old-timers don't mince words with newcomers who aren't ready to stop using: "Go back out and try some more if you haven't had enough." Old-timers don't pity newcomers. While they understand the fear and pain, they also know that pity will kill because pity leads to self-pity and eventually back to using.

So if old-timers seem harsh it's out of loving, knowing hearts—it's out of tough love.

Have I stopped pitying myself (and others)?

Higher Power, help me avoid self-pity so I can do what I need to do to recover.

Today I will avoid self-pity by

God help me to stay clean and sober today!

Making progress

As addicts, we have a disease; as *recovering* addicts it is important for us to recognize that we are getting better. It is exciting and encouraging to see how we are changing.

We are sick, but we are getting better. For example, it used to be that every time something went wrong, we *had* to run; now we just *want* to run. The running feeling is still there, but we now have a choice. Later, by the grace of God, we may not even want to run.

Can I see the progress I am making?

Higher Power, while I know there is always room for improvement, help me see the progress I have already made.

I will seek to improve myself today by

God help me to stay clean and sober today!

JULY 28

Testing the fellowship

Early in recovery, we may find ourselves testing the fellowship to see how much others will respond to us. Out of fear, anxiety, loneliness, or frustration, we may act out. But as wonderful as our fellowship is, it's not a permanent bond; it will not hold up against repeated assaults and excessive demands.

When fellowship members have had enough, they may frankly object. We may feel hurt and rejected. If we then overreact and reject the fellowship, we lose. And so does the fellowship. We need to learn what issues we have along with chemical dependency and how to deal with them. We need to learn that the fellowship needs the care and respect we'd give any relationship.

Am I treating the fellowship and myself well?

> Higher Power, help me understand
> my individual issues and to
> get help with them.

*Today I will show respect for myself
and the fellowship by*

God help me to stay clean and sober today!

Looking for answers

We are learning that the geographical cure does not guarantee staying clean and sober. As the saying has it, no matter where you go, there you are. We are learning that it's better to look for the answers in ourselves and our program than in a different city or country.

No person, place, or thing will keep us clean and sober. Recovery is in our program, in our hearts, and in the "still small voice within."

Do I know where to look for answers?

Higher Power, help me see that
I will find answers only in my soul
and not in distant places.

Today I will look within by

God help me to stay clean and sober today!

Realizing the consequences

No matter who we are as individuals, we all bear the consequences of our lifestyle and behavior. High, we experience pain, suffering, grief, and eventually insanity or premature death. Clean and sober, we experience rewarding lives.

Getting clean and sober doesn't mean that we suddenly become conformists. But whoever or whatever we become, we must practice kindness and tolerance. If we do, our lives will be meaningful in ways we cannot imagine.

Am I fully aware of the consequences of my choices?

> Higher Power, help me become
> more thoughtful and patient.

Today I will take stock of my lifestyle by

God help me to stay clean and sober today!

JULY 31

Using the phone

There are times when it seems that nothing can stop us from reaching for that first fix, pill, or drink. At times like these, it helps to reach for the phone.

Regardless of the time, day or night, we need to call our sponsor or another addict in recovery. It's critical to call them *before*, not after, we use. Many are the times that such a call has saved all we have gained in the program.

Do I make good use of the phone?

Higher Power, may I not feel too shy
or embarrassed to use the phone
when in need.

Today I will call

God help me to stay clean and sober today!

AUGUST 1

Following the leader

Whether in the program, church, or any other organization, any mortal leader we may have is but an instrument. Should any of these leaders die, our true leader remains (as always).

If we allow the absence of any person to turn us away from our Higher Power, we don't know who our real leader is. If we allow the absence of any person to halt our spiritual progress or prevent us from doing what we know is right, we are not following our true leader, our Higher Power. All others are but temporary instruments.

Am I following my true leader faithfully?

Higher Power, help me recognize
and acknowledge my true leader.

*I will share my faith in my
Higher Power today by*

God help me to stay clean and sober today!

Developing spiritually

We read in the Big Book that no human power could have relieved our addiction— not ourselves, our spouse, the law, clergy, counselors, or friends. Through trial and error and many failures, we *come to know* that another human being is not the way. To recover, we need a spiritual program based on a power greater than ourselves.

To recover, we need a spiritual life, as developed by the fellowship and the Twelve Steps.

Am I growing spiritually?

Higher Power, help me to see the importance of developing a spiritual life.

I will work on my spiritual program today by

God help me to stay clean and sober today!

Preserving and affirming our lives

Some people seem to have no problems using mood-altering drugs, but for us, they are highly destructive. When we used drugs, we lost our lives—physically and spiritually—and barely regained them through the Twelve Step program.

We who have abused mood-altering chemicals, we who are chemically dependent, must never use them again—or we risk relapse to full-blown addiction. Our path is one of total abstinence through the program.

Am I preserving and affirming my life?

Higher Power, help me to preserve
my life by staying clean and sober.

*I will affirm my life and practice
my program today by*

God help me to stay clean and sober today!

Being lucky

Some people think "luck" is the reason for success in their lives. But does luck really mean the suffering and pain that we've not hesitated to endure? The opportunities for growth that we've embraced? The kindness and humor that we've shown others? The thanks we've expressed to others for their kindness to us?

If success is "lucky," then we make our own luck. Then luck means being open and available; luck means willingness plus grace.

Do I realize what a lucky person I am?

> Higher Power, help me to be open
> and willing to receive your grace.

Today I will thank God for my "luck" by

God help me to stay clean and sober today!

Accepting change

In recovery, we have much work to do and many lessons to learn as we mend our ways and relationships. Each time we change we grow stronger and freer.

But often we are so attached to our defects and dependencies we are afraid of change, even good change. As suggested in Step Six, our job is to become willing to let change happen when the time is right.

Am I becoming willing to change?

> Higher Power, help me to accept the need for change and to fear it less.

I am willing to change today by

God help me to stay clean and sober today!

Twelfth-Stepping

Our addictive personalities can produce un-expected twists in character: Many of us can't stand practicing addicts of any kind. It feels old to Twelfth-Step someone who reminds us so sharply of where we came from. Who wants to get up at three o'clock in the morning to Twelfth-Step someone who's high and probably won't remember what you said anyway?

What's the use? we may ask. *We're* the use! Twelfth-Stepping is something we need to do to stay clean and sober. We may not like it all the time, but it keeps us growing.

Do I always carry the message to those who still suffer?

> God give me the strength, patience,
> and love it requires to Twelfth-Step
> those who still suffer.

Today I will work on tolerance by

God help me to stay clean and sober today!

Getting past the differences

Although the language of the Twelve Step program may sound religious at times, its goals are entirely spiritual. Whether we hold atheistic, Christian, Jewish, Muslim, or other beliefs, we are welcome in the fellowship.

To take part, all we need to do is accept that we have addiction we cannot handle on our own and accept that a power greater than ourselves can help.

Can I take what I like from the program and leave the rest?

Higher Power, help me see what I share
with others in the program and to
let go of the differences.

*Today I will decide what I like,
and dislike, about the program by*

God help me to stay clean and sober today!

Recovering love

Our Higher Power has always loved us and always will. Our problem is learning to accept and believe that. While using mood-altering chemicals, we were unable to accept this love. Later, we could not even believe in this love. And for many of us, the same problems are true in our other relationships.

By getting free of mood-altering chemicals, by getting into recovery and going to Twelve Step meetings, we will see love in action. We will see that it is real and can be trusted. We will feel its power to heal and make whole.

Am I experiencing love again?

Higher Power, help me to absorb the love that flows in the fellowship.

Today I will be especially loving toward

God help me to stay clean and sober today!

Admitting unmanageability

"What do you mean, 'unmanageable'?" we ask when we first come into the program. (And we are surprised at the smiling faces and suppressed chuckles.) We have been living with our delusions for so long that we really believe everything is okay—or will be okay *next* week. We simply can't see how out of control our lives truly are: angry creditors, unemployment, separation or divorce, health problems.

Some of these situations were ridiculous, others tragic—and *still* we fantasized that we were in control. After a period of time in the program, however, living with them seems hard to imagine. But if we still think we have control, we need to ask for help in facing our delusions and our tomorrow-will-be-better syndrome.

Have I turned the management of my life over to God?

Higher Power, help me to
truly accept Step One.

*I will look at what is
unmanageable in my life today by*

God help me to stay clean and sober today!

Adapting to the world

"Live only in today; don't worry about tomorrow." That's a fine ambition, we may think, but what does it mean? "Living in today" means dealing only with what is at hand *now* and the available courses of action.

If we are worrying about matters in the past or future, or out of our realm, we can disengage ourselves from them. We cannot bend the world to our will.

Am I learning to fit myself to the world?

> Higher Power, help me remember
> to conquer myself, not the world.

*Today I will practice adapting myself
to whatever happens by*

Listening to the heart

What we truly want for ourselves comes from the heart, not from the head. Our head only *thinks* it knows what's important.

Because it brought relief from some of our pain, we *thought* addiction was what we wanted. But eventually our heart told us that *addiction is painful* and that relief is in recovery, sobriety, and the fellowship.

Am I learning to think twice and see what my heart is saying?

Higher Power, help me to listen to my heart when matters are most important.

Today I will pay close attention to my feelings by

God help me to stay clean and sober today!

Becoming virtuous

For some of us, becoming virtuous means bringing our behavior in line with a Higher Will. It means acting in line with our deepest convictions—not necessarily religious doctrines, nor the ideas drummed into our heads in childhood, nor the beliefs of virtuous people.

For some of us, this means that we have some work to do: We must find out what we believe in, and then we must live by those beliefs.

Do I know my beliefs? Do I live by them?

> Higher Power, help me discover
> what I truly believe in.

Today I will live my deepest beliefs by

God help me to stay clean and sober today!

Preserving anonymity

Anonymity means more than just protecting fellow members from exposure or shame. It means placing principles above personalities. It means avoiding the temptation to use our recovery as a prestige point. Such self-seeking can be a serious spiritual danger.

Our program is our lifeline. We must respect it and all its members. Do I maintain anonymity at all times, in all ways?

> Higher Power, help me to accept
> and respect the traditions
> of the Twelve Step program.

> *Today I will reflect on the
> tradition of anonymity by*

God help me to stay clean and sober today!

Keeping our program in mind

In the heat of summer, it can be hard to re-member that we have meetings to attend and a program to work. When we think we are too busy to get to meetings or to work the Steps, our minds are beginning to slip. The pull of mood-altering chemicals can be felt in laziness, boredom, or uncomfortable circumstances.

At times like these, it is important to re-member how we got straight and what keeps us straight.

Do I keep my program in mind at all times?

Higher Power, help me prevent anything from interfering with my crucial Twelve Step program.

Today I will practice my program by

God help me to stay clean and sober today!

AUGUST 15

Sharing our burdens

We were disappointed in ourselves when we could not rise above situations that enveloped us. We were discouraged with friends who seemed indifferent to our suffering.

But coming to the program, we find that we need not fear the burdens of life. Our Higher Power has given us examples, promises, and friends to share all our burdens. For example, with understanding people we find that we need never be alone again.

Do I share all my crosses with my fellows and with my Creator?

> Higher Power, help me to realize
> that there are others on my path
> and to believe that they can help.

The burden I will share today is

God help me to stay clean and sober today!

Persuading others

This is a program of attraction, not promotion. It's not necessary to persuade people to see things our way. If our new lives—clean, sober, and serene—are not enough to attract others, then they have not yet suffered enough to want help.

We are instructed simply to carry the message. Our Higher Power will put us in position to help others and put others in position to be helped. It then becomes their choice—to reach out for help or turn away.

Have I let go of helping others until they want help from me?

Higher Power, help me to remember
that my job is only to carry the message.

Today I will be available with the message for

God help me to stay clean and sober today!

Pausing for HALT

The acronym HALT reminds us to avoid getting too hungry, angry, lonely, or tired. When we feel this way for a while, we are much more likely to have a slip or to relapse.

When we feel especially hungry, angry, lonely, or tired, it helps to pause and attend to what our bodies and spirits are telling us they need. We will be happier and more serene when we can avoid their extremes.

Do I pause when I feel too H? A? L? T?

Higher Power, help me to become more aware of the needs of my body and spirit.

If I feel especially hungry, angry, lonely, or tired today, I will

God help me to stay clean and sober today!

Adjusting and coping

Many of us in recovery do not like the idea of having to adjust and cope. We have "controlled" our lives for so many years, it's hard to believe that the world does not revolve around us. But it doesn't. And we can see now that forcing situations to suit ourselves inevitably leaves other people "unsuited" and unhappy.

The good news may not seem to make sense at first. If we find ways to adjust and cope, our lives will actually get easier. Things will go our way more often. We will experience less stress, both externally and internally. We will experience harmony.

Am I learning to adjust and cope?

Higher Power, help me to
want what I have.

Today I will adjust to, or cope with,
others' wants or needs by

AUGUST 19

Feeling self-important

After being in the program for a while, some of us feel we know much more than the average member (and perhaps we do). But self-importance helps no one. What is important is working hard to stay clean and sober. By taking care of ourselves, we quietly set a good example.

We need to carry the message and offer help, but it does not help to set ourselves above or apart.

Am I letting go of any self-importance?

> Higher Power, help me to learn
> my weaknesses and be humble.

I will practice humility today by

God help me to stay clean and sober today!

Growing slowly

Our Higher Power has a divine plan for each of us. It may take awhile for us to understand our place in it, however. We may not know what we are supposed to do; we only know what we're *not* to do. We may feel empty at times. If during these painfully slow times, we can have faith that things will change, we can learn to endure the uncertainty with less fear.

During such times it may seem to us that nothing is happening. But just as mountains finally emerged from the restless terrain, so will growth emerge in our lives after a period of stress. Growth can emerge only if we are patient.

Is my faith strong enough for slow and steady growth?

> Higher Power, help me to be patient
> and faithful in this time of
> unsteady change and steady growth.

Today I will strengthen my faith by

AUGUST 21

Practicing tolerance

Everyone has a different opinion. No two people look the same. We all are different. Differences can cause us fear and set us apart from others, and we have no idea why.

If addiction closes us down, recovery opens us up. In the program, we learn that we are all more alike than we are different. We learn to look for what we share. We learn that we know so little about ourselves (let alone others) and that judgments are not helpful.

Can I live and let live?

> Higher Power, help me
> to see myself in others.

I will practice tolerance today by

God help me to stay clean and sober today!

Letting go

If addiction is about control, recovery is about *letting go*. If addiction is about denial, recovery is about *accepting what is*.

As we spend time in the program, we learn something unexpected and amazing: Life is so full of twists and turns, it's easier to follow along than to try to straighten them out. It's easier to have fewer expectations because, after all, we have no control over the future *or* the present.

Can I practice letting go?

Higher Power, help me to be open,
flexible, and accepting in my recovery.

*Today I will let others make decisions
and let go of*

God help me to stay clean and sober today!

Treasuring our triumph

It is said that the tougher the problem, the greater the triumph. Some of us feel that we would gladly have forgone the conflict *and* the triumph. If that is how we're thinking, we have not fully experienced the triumph.

Our lives have ultimate value. Getting clean and sober after years of addictive living is an amazing and wonderful achievement. It is also said that heaven knows the proper price of its goods.

Can I realize the full value of what I have done?

Higher Power, help me to love and respect myself for the life-saving work I have done.

*I will express my gratitude
for my being clean and sober today by*

God help me to stay clean and sober today!

Seeking a Higher Power

In the Twelve Step program, Step Two suggests that we seek a Higher Power (whom some of us choose to call God) to help us with the problems that we can't handle alone. And here some of us—for very old and deep reasons—get stuck.

God need not be male, nor old and bearded. God need not be judgmental or punishing. The fact is, in the Twelve Step program we can let go of our old notions about God. The fact is, *we can decide* what we want our Higher Power to be to get the help we need.

Can I begin seeking a Higher Power?

I now realize I have a serious problem.
I see that I cannot recover on my own.
I need help.

*Today I will begin to explore
my spiritual beliefs by*

God help me to stay clean and sober today!

AUGUST 25

Being in trouble

Many of us have experienced failure in school, loss of jobs, quarrels with families and friends, and encounters with police and jails. In the beginning it is hard to realize that trouble is not simply a part of our personality. We may feel jinxed.

But through the program we realize that we don't have to live that way. We don't have to feel jinxed. We can finally see what "peace of mind" means.

Am I leaving my troubles behind me?

Higher Power, help me to realize
all the choices I now have in my life.

I will enhance my peace of mind today by

God help me to stay clean and sober today!

Letting go of fear

Some people talk about the Four Horsemen of chemical dependency: Terror, Bewilderment, Frustration, and Despair. The Four Horsemen have a leader, Fear, and there are a thousand forms of fear for the horsemen to command.

The way to combat the horsemen and their leader is with abstinence, honesty, and faith (fear cannot exist where there is faith).

Am I finding the faith to let go of my fear?

Higher Power, help me find
the faith I need to let go of fear.

*Should I feel afraid about anything today,
I will pray that*

God help me to stay clean and sober today!

Dealing with depression

When we felt depressed, we used to take the "quickest" escape route: getting high or drunk. But we found that we couldn't escape feelings for very long and that using drugs or alcohol leaves us feeling no better, and often worse, both physically and emotionally.

At times like these, it would be more useful if we could avoid trying to escape the feelings and avoid the chemicals. It would be more useful to remember our Higher Power, the program, and our fellow members.

Can I use the program to help deal with feelings of depression?

Higher Power, when I feel depressed,
help me to use my program, avoid
self-medication, and to reach out for help.

*I will practice dealing with
feelings of depression today by*

God help me to stay clean and sober today!

Maintaining conscious contact

At meetings, it's fairly easy to be in touch with our Higher Power, but it's the rest of the time that's most important, time when we face our problems on our own. It helps if we can work the program throughout the day, to keep in conscious contact with our Higher Power.

Many of us use the Serenity Prayer. Others use personal prayers, meditate, or set aside quiet moments during the day.

Do I have a way to hook up with my Higher Power?

Higher Power, help me to make the time to maintain conscious contact with you.

Today I will improve my conscious contact with God by

God help me to stay clean and sober today!

Working the Twelve Steps

There is a good reason why the Twelve Steps are numbered one to twelve: They are meant to be taken in order. For instance, we must admit we are powerless over our addiction (Step One) before the other steps can help us. Likewise, Step Four would be too painful if we had not turned our wills and our lives over to the care of God in Step Three. And how can we make amends in Steps Eight and Nine unless we realize whom we have hurt in Steps Four and Five? Of course, we can do Step Twelve only after doing all the other Steps.

The hop-skip-jump method of working the Steps is not reliable and might hop-skip-jump us right back into our addiction.

Do I work all Twelve Steps of the program in the best order?

Higher Power, give me the strength
to take each Step—as hard as it may be—
in the most helpful order.

*Today I will review my progress on each of the
Steps and re-enter the order with*

God help me to stay clean and sober today!

AUGUST 30

*Accepting others
(and ourselves)*

We must guard against judging other people:
As we judge, so are we judged. In other
words, if we keep thinking that others will
slip, we are more likely to slip ourselves.

It seems that unconsciously we try to feel
better about our own character defects by
projecting them onto others. If we practice
accepting ourselves, however, we will be better able to accept others.

To help this practice, we must realize that
our defects will be removed by our Higher
Power in time, as long as we desire and pray
that they be removed. We must also realize
that we are not perfect and that we need and
deserve love.

Can I fully accept myself and others?

**Higher Power, help me to accept others
by working on self-acceptance.**

*I will work on what I find difficult to accept
in myself today by*

God help me to stay clean and sober today!

Accepting misfortune

We all know that misfortune, great or small, is a part of life. But what we may not realize is that it involves both defeat *and* victory.

The defeat involves knowing that we can't change the results; the victory involves letting go of control and knowing that our Higher Power will always help us carry our burdens.

Am I learning to accept misfortune?

Higher Power, help me to accept the fact that there is great mystery in life.

Today I will work on accepting my misfortune by

God help me to stay clean and sober today!

SEPTEMBER 1

Coming to believe

Many of us come to the Twelve Step program with little or no belief in a Higher Power. Perhaps we tried religion and it didn't help, or perhaps we prefer science to religion. In either event, we need not turn away from the program; what we need is support until we can take Step Two.

It will help if we can see that alcohol and other drugs can no longer be our Higher Power, that we cannot recover on our own, and that a Higher Power may be anything that helps us stay clean and sober.

Can I find something to believe in?

I know I need help. I want to find someone or something in which I can put my faith.

Today I will look for a Higher Power by

God help me to stay clean and sober today!

SEPTEMBER 2

Practicing spiritual principles

Just exactly what can we do to put our spiritual principles into practice? Here are some ideas.

We can say *love* when others say *hate*. We can say *people* when others say *money*. We can speak up when others are silent. We can carry on when others give up. We can offer help when others withdraw. We can follow the program while others search for a softer way.

How active is my spiritual life?

Higher Power, help me find the courage to practice my spiritual principles.

The spiritual principle I will practice today is

God help me to stay clean and sober today!

SEPTEMBER 3

Giving tough love

We need to support those who still suffer, but it doesn't help to pity them. That's unfair.

To get well, they need to know exactly what they're up against and what they need to do. They need the whole story about addiction and the hope of recovery.

Can I be candid and caring at the same time?

Higher Power, help me to see how
I can best help those who still suffer.

*Today I will practice being
honest and direct by*

God help me to stay clean and sober today!

Coping with fear

After getting clean and sober, we may suddenly become very fearful. Situations that never bothered us in our using days loom up at us. Some of us feel terror when riding with a careless driver. Some of us feel panicky at the thought of a burglar. Some of us fear losing our jobs for no good reason.

As we regain our sanity, we may feel our lives become extraordinarily valuable. This is good, but it will help if we can practice trusting in our Higher Power and the fellowship.

In time, our fears will diminish.

Am I learning to handle fear?

Higher Power, help me to believe that my process is normal and that I am not alone.

I will deal with my fear today by

God help me to stay clean and sober today!

Practicing abstinence

We must always remember that *absolute* abstinence is the keystone to our recovery. Using any mood-altering chemicals will prevent us from working the program effectively. They flip our thinking back into old patterns and eventually con us back into full-blown addiction.

There are many products we must be careful of: antihistamines, cough syrups, over-the-counter sleeping pills, caffeine tablets, and others. If we experience addiction and compulsions, we must be extremely careful about what we put into our mouths.

Am I staying absolutely clean?

Higher Power, help me to accept
my addiction and the need to abstain
from any mood-altering chemicals.

I will strengthen my abstinence today by

God help me to stay clean and sober today!

Dealing with now

When we were using, we kept avoiding the present moment (it was too painful) by using mood-altering chemicals. Clean and sober, we see that right now is all we have. If we avoid *it*, we avoid *life*.

Whether it's getting to school or work, taking care of other daily duties, or staying clean and sober, am I doing what I need to be doing right now?

Higher Power, help me be strong enough
to do what I need to do right now.

Today I will improve my level of awareness by

God help me to stay clean and sober today!

Finding the common bond

We are one among so many and may feel "terminally unique." We need help; we need each other.

If we see that we're all in the same boat, that we're more alike than different, we can diminish whatever seems to separate us. Then we can offer each other our experience, strength, and hope.

Can I look for the common bond?

Higher Power, help me find
what I share with my fellow travelers.

*To make a connection
with one other person today,
I will*

God help me to stay clean and sober today!

Feeling the joy

Through this program we learn to live, we learn to work, we learn to play. We learn to be happy alone or with others. We learn love, and the result is joy.

This joy in living sets us free: Our choices expand; what was out of reach before now comes into our reach. Recovering in the program is a form of walking joy.

Am I experiencing and expressing joy?

> Higher Power, help me to see
> the great change in my life,
> to feel the joy.

Today I will express my joy by

Letting go of pain

When we focus on positive thoughts, resentment and fear can hardly touch us. Positive thoughts protect us and lead us forward.

When our minds are full of negative thoughts, we suffer; negative thoughts make us vulnerable and hold us back. Do we really want to suffer?

Can I practice letting go of pain?

> Higher Power, help me believe that
> letting go of pain
> really does bring relief.

Today I will practice letting go of pain by

God help me to stay clean and sober today!

Comparing

We are proud of the fact that if someone wants to join the program, sex, age, race, status, sexual orientation, or religious preferences do not matter. Yet we may still find ourselves judging the kind or severity of another's addiction.

How can we possibly judge another's pain? Or problems? Or recovery needs? And why bother? Don't we have enough pain and problems of our own?

Have I stopped judging others?

> Higher Power, help me to
> see that comparing separates
> me from myself and others.

*I will practice accepting all my
fellow travelers in recovery today by*

God help me to stay clean and sober today!

Making mistakes

As addicts we made a lot of mistakes; as addicts, we blanketed those mistakes in denial. Clean and sober, denial is no longer an option. Yet we still make plenty of mistakes.

But mistakes are okay, because we're learning that every situation, good or bad, is an opportunity for growth. And with the right attitude, we can make the most of it.

Can I let go of my mistakes enough to learn from them?

Higher Power, help me to
forgive my mistakes and to
accept them as a useful way to learn.

*Today I will practice what I learned from
my most recent mistake by*

God help me to stay clean and sober today!

SEPTEMBER 12

Avoiding intellectual pride

Intellectual pride can be a great downfall for those of us with addiction. We shouldn't con ourselves into thinking that program guidelines don't apply to "smart" people. Besides, if we're so smart, how did we end up here in the first place?

Whether we finish high school or college, whether our collar is blue or white, all aspects of this program apply to us. Until we realize that the solution to our problem is our common bond—not our training, job, or lifestyle—we will make little progress. Our problem is no respecter of persons, but our solution is valid for all.

Can I keep my "smarts" from getting in my way?

Higher Power, help me realize
that intellectual pride can
prevent me from working my program.

Today I will practice humility by

God help me to stay clean and sober today!

SEPTEMBER 13

Developing a sense of humor

We may not believe this, but it helps to think that life isn't strictly serious. There's much humor in it and a sense of humor often eases pain. If we can laugh, chances are we can forgive both ourselves and others.

It may not feel like it, but recovery isn't strictly serious either. Getting clean and sober (and helping others do the same) is often a process full of joy.

Can I find something to laugh at today?

Higher Power, help me see the humor
in all my seriousness, help me laugh.

Today I will work on my sense of humor by

God help me to stay clean and sober today!

Being patient

Over time, we get what we want out of this program. If we seek a better way of life, for example, we will develop it. If we want to diminish our pain, we will find relief. If we want love, we will learn how to give it and receive it.

Over time, our lives can improve a great deal through the Twelve Step program. Thus, our job is to keep coming to meetings and working the Steps.

Can I do what I need to do to get what I want?

Higher Power, help me to be
patient with myself, the program,
and the process of change.

I will continue my process of recovery today by

God help me to stay clean and sober today!

Learning how to pray

Step Eleven may give us concern: *I haven't prayed in so many years! What do I do? I don't even know where to begin.*

Fortunately, praying can be as simple as it is important. It need not be long or formal. It needs no particular prayer, time, or place. It is simply thinking good thoughts, saying our feelings, or reviewing our day. Whatever we do as praying is a good thing.

Am I learning how to pray?

> Higher Power, help me pray.
> Help me stay in touch with
> my spiritual self.

Today I will pray by

God help me to stay clean and sober today!

Letting go of guilt

Once in the grips of addiction, we used mood-altering chemicals less because we wanted to than because we were hooked. We hurt ourselves and others less because we wanted to than because we were hooked. We felt guilty, and as our disease progressed, guilt overwhelmed us.

Being clean and sober, we need to let go of this crippling guilt along with our insane past. To do this, we use Steps Four and Five. As we work these soul-cleansing Steps, we forgive ourselves. By forgiving ourselves, we come to love ourselves and so become able to love others.

Am I letting go of guilt?

Higher Power, help me to
work the Steps and forgive myself.

*If I feel guilty about something today,
I will practice forgiving myself by*

God help me to stay clean and sober today!

Letting go

Some of us who abused mood-altering chemicals have been urged to change our behavior by using "willpower" or by "resisting temptation." It's a common misconception that we should be masters of our souls.

But if addiction is a disease of control, recovery is about letting go. Ironically, only when we realize that we don't know how to be masters—how did we end up here in the first place?—can we progress. We may not know exactly what to do to recover or how to do it, but we know we have help in the program.

Am I trusting my life and will over to my Higher Power?

> Higher Power, help me to believe
> that letting go is more freeing
> than frightening.

To practice letting go today, I will

God help me to stay clean and sober today!

Resolving to stay clean and sober

When we first dry out and get clean, it's a good idea to make ninety meetings in ninety days: Our minds are still in a haze. We need extra meetings and extra support in the very beginning.

It took a lot of denial and time to hit bottom. To climb back up the hill we've just come down, it will take a lot of *acceptance* and time.

Have I made the commitment to staying clean and sober?

> Higher Power, help me work as hard
> at staying clean and sober as I did
> at using chemicals.

> *I will commit myself to staying
> clean and sober today by*

God help me to stay clean and sober today!

Being human

We are imperfect, human. To learn, we make mistakes and suffer consequences. This is true for all of us, everywhere.

So when we do very human things, it helps if we do not punish ourselves but accept our humanness. We need not judge ourselves as others might, but only as God might judge us, with complete acceptance.

Am I learning to accept my humanness?

Higher Power, help me to see that my humanness is less a problem than a path.

Today I will celebrate my humanness by

God help me to stay clean and sober today!

Changing

The old saying is true: You can lead a horse to water but you can't make it drink. It's the same with addiction and recovery. People can take away our drugs and put us in treatment, but no one can *make* us clean and sober.

When it hurts enough, when we're scared enough, when we're sick and tired enough, when we've lost enough, then we'll begin to change. But we have to *want* to change. It's the key.

What am I willing to do to recover?

Higher Power, help me to want
what I need, to want what is best for me.

I will further my recovery today by

God help me to stay clean and sober today!

Choosing the spiritual life

As we come into recovery, we have a critical choice to make. We can choose either the spiritual world (the Twelve Steps) or the material world (which we already know hasn't worked for us). We can choose to live in the spirit or to live in an illusion (part of which was our addiction).

We can put our faith in a Higher Power or we can follow (and fear) the opinions of others. We can make a commitment, or we can be passive and withdrawn.

Which choice strengthens my recovery?

Higher Power, help me to always choose the path that keeps my recovery strong.

As part of my spiritual life, today I will

God help me to stay clean and sober today!

Seeking truth

As addicts, we were sure we knew the truth, but we didn't. We knew very little about truth but a lot about the lie of addiction.

In recovery, we want to find out what is true for us. We do this by listening carefully to others, asking questions, and then slowly deciding for ourselves.

Am I seeking the truth?

Higher Power, help me to be
open to new truths and strong enough
to apply them in my life.

Today I will be authentic by

God help me to stay clean and sober today!

Waking up to life

Even in recovery, it is hard for many of us to avoid old habits that keep us from making the most of our lives. For instance, there is love withheld, people and experiences avoided, dreams ignored. Even avoiding pain diminished the richness of life.

Now that we have taken back our lives, we can practice living more of it. We can make some changes, accept a few challenges, take some risks. There is so much to be gained.

Am I waking up to life?

> Higher Power, help me to develop
> the course to embrace my life
> and make the most of it.

Today I will live life to the fullest by

God help me to stay clean and sober today!

Learning

It seems as if we're particularly immature, especially in the early stages of recovery. When we were using, we handled all of our problems the same way: When faced with difficult relationships, we used chemicals. When faced with responsibilities, we used chemicals. When faced with life, we used chemicals. Chemicals took the place of learning experiences.

Fortunately, we're clean and sober now, and we can learn from our problems. We are more mature now that we understand our strengths and weaknesses better, and we know how to work the program to recover.

Am I learning from my experiences?

**Higher Power, help me to be strong
(enough) to evaluate and learn
from my mistakes.**

Today I will practice learning by

God help me to stay clean and sober today!

Overcoming strong desire

Desire—especially strong desire—is a kind of mental fever. It seems to put us in a weaker position. There is desire for money, for power, for prestige, and for mood-altering chemicals.

When desire is strong, we operate out of a haze. We lose good judgment. We must never let desire come before our program.

Am I dealing with my strong desires?

Higher Power, help me to let go of
any strong desire that might
weaken my recovery.

*Today I will deal with any of my
strong desires by*

God help me to stay clean and sober today!

SEPTEMBER 26

Being open to new ideas

Some of us get stuck in the past, in tradition. While there is great wisdom in all who have come before us, that's not all there is. Even if we believe that there are no new ideas, new writers can help us because they understand our culture, they speak our language.

Consider this: At one time—perhaps recently—the Twelve Step program was a new idea to us.

Can I be receptive to new ideas?

Higher Power, help me see that I will be happier and progress faster if I stay open and flexible in my thinking.

To stay open in my thinking today, I will

God help me to stay clean and sober today!

Thinking positively

Because of our history with alcohol and other drugs, it's probably a lot easier for us—or a lot more familiar—to think about the negative, to think about our problems, about what's wrong with us or the world. It's pretty easy for negative thoughts to lead to more negative thoughts; it's a lot harder for negative thoughts to lead to positive thoughts. Of course, change is not easy.

Let's not be too simplistic about this, but having an upbeat attitude—thinking positive thoughts—really does help. As tough as it is to do sometimes, if we can concentrate on what's working for us, or what small but helpful change we made the other day, things will get better.

Can I think positively (even when I don't feel all that positive)?

Higher Power, help me to see more of the light instead of—so often—the dark.

I will focus on the positive today by

God help me to stay clean and sober today!

SEPTEMBER 28

Keeping the faith

For many of us, the spiritual crisis of addiction probably meant an overwhelming loss of faith in ourselves and the world.

But in recovery we see that life becomes a lot easier with faith in a Higher Power. For example, failure, loss, and death are no less painful, but with a Higher Power, we don't feel quite as alone, we don't feel as if we've lost everything. With faith, things seem to have more meaning.

Am I keeping the faith?

Higher Power, help me to accept my spiritual doubts and still carry on.

I will strengthen my faith today by

God help me to stay clean and sober today!

Taking things in stride

When we first begin to recover—feel a connection to our Higher Power, work the first three Steps, and begin to change—we might feel grateful, giddy, self-conscious, happy, proud, and special, among others.

It may seem odd, but some people may react negatively to us. They may look at us with jealousy, irritation, shame, skepticism, or mistrust. But it makes sense: We're different and they don't know quite what to make of us yet. It helps if we can be aware of this and not overreact, just keep up our good work and trust that it will all get resolved in time.

Can I have faith and stay focused?

Higher Power, help me to relax
and take others' reactions
to my changes in stride.

I will focus on my own recovery today by

God help me to stay clean and sober today!

Praying

There are different ways to pray and different things to pray about. We can use words or we can pray silently through careful, mindful, spiritual acts. We can pray for ourselves or others, for what we need or want, or we can pray to follow the will of our Higher Power.

In fact, we can make a prayer out of most anything we do. The *way* we do what we do can make most any act a prayer.

Am I staying in conscious contact through my prayers?

Higher Power, help me to keep prayer,
whether spoken or silent,
an active part of my spiritual life.

I will keep up my prayer life today by

God help me to stay clean and sober today!

OCTOBER 1

Helping others

We can arm ourselves with a lot of facts about mind-altering chemicals to share with addicts, but just hearing the information will not necessarily convince anyone of their addiction. We cannot prance around diagnosing people, but we can make suggestions that encourage users to diagnose themselves.

We can propose the "controlled using for thirty days" test or one of the several written self-tests. If they pass the tests, then their problem is probably not like ours. We are not doctors or demigods, but we can carry the message. When God sees fit, there are those we can aid.

Do I try to help others diagnose themselves?

Higher Power, may your love and light shine forth through me, but may I not set myself up to do your job.

Today I will carry the message to

God help me to stay clean and sober today!

Learning about love

Being straight, we are discovering the joys of love. Just as our old ideas about living had to change, our old ideas about love have to change. Love can't always be measured by self-sacrifice or generosity. We can self-sacrifice ourselves into martyrdom or generosity ourselves into directing and managing others' lives.

Love doesn't stipulate or limit. Does our Higher Power limit us? It loves us so much that it lets us go *over* the limit—to the point where we destroy ourselves. Few of us know much about the true nature of love, but when we are ready, our Higher Power reveals itself to us and shows us about love.

Have I learned all about love?

May I know with all my heart
that my Higher Power *is* love.

*Today I will make myself ready
to learn about love by*

God help me to stay clean and sober today!

Sharing ourselves

We can't give away what we don't have, but what can we give? Ourselves. We do this by sharing our experience, strength, and hope. Whether we share with an individual or a group, we are walking, talking miracles of what our program can do.

But this program works only through our Higher Power, and only through our Higher Power can we have the joy of sharing with others.

Do I share myself wholly with those who seek help?

> Higher Power, meet and defeat
> the hostile forces in me that I
> may bring your glory to others.

Today I will share myself wholeheartedly with

God help me to stay clean and sober today!

Trying to escape

In an attempt to get out of the box we found ourselves in, many of us tried the geographic escape. We moved from place to place. Invariably, we found ourselves in pretty much the same, if not a worse, situation.

We knew we had real emotional and material problems, but we weren't aware that using chemicals was actually causing much of our distress. The chemicals induced a state of mind that led to behavior patterns that wouldn't have occurred had we not been "out of our minds."

Have I stopped trying to escape?

Higher Power, help me to know
that it's not my location that makes
the difference in my life, it's
what I'm working with inside.

*Today, instead of seeking escape,
I will try to improve my situation by*

God help me to stay clean and sober today!

Becoming detached

In our need to become a whole person, we sometimes find it necessary to project an environment we believe will be more satisfactory than our present one: a different town, a new position, or a profitable goal. But if we don't remember that we have no power over our own life, these dreams can become pitfalls.

If we forget our powerlessness and start desperately seeking a goal or a place, we open ourselves to discouragement and disillusionment. But if we truly detach—by turning our will and our lives over to our Higher Power's care—we will achieve real happiness through our Higher Power.

Do I give the future to my Higher Power?

Higher Power, I pray that when I look
farther ahead than today, you will
help me to be where it is best for me to be.

*The goals and aspirations I will
hand over to my High Power today are*

God help me to stay clean and sober today!

OCTOBER 6

Finding our path

We are the result of what we have applied. In recovery we have a chance to apply new principles to our lives. In doing so, we are able to abandon old habits and ideas and, bit by bit, to recognize our Higher Power's plan for us.

Cleaning house is a necessary beginning for our new way of life. Every day, instead of following our ego's will, we can take the cues given by our Higher Power and use them to stay connected to our spiritual path in life.

Have I become what I'm meant to be?

Higher Power, today may I
begin practicing, thinking, and living
according to your plan for me.

*I will allow my Higher Power
to guide me on my path today by*

God help me to stay clean and sober today!

Making the stretch

Some of us come into the program and are gung ho for the first three to six weeks. We're like a quarter horse, good for the short run but not for the long stretch. After we come down from the high of winning our first run, reality and responsibility seep in and we step out, possibly even give up.

So something has to carry us through, and that is our Higher Power, providing we let it. Then, as time passes, we find we no longer feel the need to use drugs. Our Higher Power is what guides us through.

Am I good for the long stretch?

> Higher Power, guide me with your
> loving light for the whole race.

Today I will improve my stamina by practicing

God help me to stay clean and sober today!

OCTOBER 8

Liking the program

Because most of us who have been around the program awhile like it here, newcomers sometimes mistakenly think that we wanted to be here. They imagine us eagerly waiting to dash into the promised land.

Ha! None of us wanted to come here at first, but how can we help it if we love it in the program now that we've found it to be a true way to solve our problems?

Do I like it here?

Higher Power, let me be grateful always for having found this new way of life, but help me remember how the newcomer feels.

Today I will enjoy the program by

God help me to stay clean and sober today!

Slipping

A common rationalization about not making the program goes like this: *Harry over there slipped ten times before he made it. So what if I slip a few times?*

What is overlooked is that the last time Jack slipped, he slipped into a coffin; the last time Bob slipped, his baby son burned to death in a crib because of Bob's negligence; the last time Ann slipped, she got strychnine poisoning and became blind; and the last time Jim slipped, he tried to kill his wife and nearly did.

We're not playing games here. This is a matter of life and death.

Have I stopped slipping?

Higher Power, let me know that it is not only my life but the lives of others that I endanger by playing loaded games.

I will avoid slipping today by

God help me to stay clean and sober today!

Growing spiritually

The physical part of our addiction is not the main factor of our illness. Many of us have had allergies to products such as milk, but we didn't have to join Milk Drinkers Anonymous because we couldn't stop. The physical part would be of little consequence if it weren't accompanied by an equally progressive spiritual deterioration.

Because the major contributing factor to substance abuse is spiritual deterioration, the emphasis in recovery is on the spiritual. That is why only two Steps mention the alcoholic and ten talk about spiritual growth.

Is my spiritual progress evident in all my actions?

> Higher Power, may the spiritual
> illumination of the Twelve Steps
> become a reality for me
> and help me grow today.

Today, my plan for living spiritually is

God help me to stay clean and sober today!

Using the program

Some nonaddicted people accuse us of using our program as a crutch. They are quick to put down what they don't understand. But let's question this reasoning. People have to work to earn a living; we have to work our program to live. Is a job a crutch?

A job is a form of support, and our fellowship is also a form of support. We need never be ashamed of our glorious fellowship, which has brought so much joy into so many lives.

Do I use the program to the fullest?

Higher Power, may I know that I do not have to justify my program, my addiction, or my existence.

Today I will use the program by

God help me to stay clean and sober today!

OCTOBER 12

Putting first things first

When we have loved ones who are also in the program, we must constantly remind ourselves where our priorities lie. We are told not to interfere in family members' programs. We have to take care of our own addiction first before attending to the affairs of others.

Once we turn our attention to loved ones, the same principle applies. We must respond to the addict in them first and then attend to other matters. Our responsibility to the addict in people must come first, or we may lose sight of our true priorities and mess up our own lives as well as theirs.

Do I put first things first?

My messages come from my Higher Power
first. May they flow through me
and then spread to loved ones
and to all other areas of my life.

Today I will reassess my priorities and

God help me to stay clean and sober today!

OCTOBER 13

People-pleasing

People-pleasing! Why do we spend so much time and energy trying to please other people? We sometimes find ourselves saying yes to every request made of us. Perhaps we try to please people in exchange for affirmation. Perhaps we feel guilty about our past and want to make up for it. Or maybe we just need to be in the limelight.

People-pleasing or being yes-people only hurts us. What is not coming from our hearts and is not done in the true spirit of loving is only another game of martyrdom or egoism. We are learning not to play these games any longer.

Do I serve others from the heart?

Higher Power, I need not please
those around me to be a nice person,
but I do need to serve others
through you in the true spirit of love.

Today I will examine my true feelings about

God help me to stay clean and sober today!

Being cured

It's easy for friends and associates to see us as people who are super-sober, super-clean. They think we have the problem licked, that we're cured. This is shown by their uneasiness when we say, "I am an alcoholic; I am an addict." They would prefer us to say, "I was."

We would like to believe them, but in our hearts we know that it's not possible for us to drink or use any longer. By saying we are addicted, we remind ourselves of who we are and where we came from.

Am I grateful for being clean and sober, even though I can never be cured?

> Higher Power, grant me the acceptance
> to understand that I am not cured.
> Relieve my temptation to believe those
> well-meaning people who are convinced
> that I am no longer an addict.

Today I will enjoy being clean and sober by

God help me to stay clean and sober today!

Being positive

For us to grow and develop spiritually, we need to examine our thoughts and beliefs. Do we look for the good in people, places, and events? Do we shed a positive light on all we come into contact with? To understand and accept is not to limit or control. Acknowledging the truth generates positive energy, positive thoughts, and a positive lifestyle.

Negative thinking produces negative ways. It undermines our morals so that we develop a "what's the difference" attitude. But a positive faith in a Higher Power, as each of us understands it, gives strength to the body and courage to the soul.

Do I have positive beliefs?

Higher Power, may positive thoughts and beliefs be the guiding forces of my life.

I will cultivate positive beliefs today by

God help me to stay clean and sober today!

Releasing our selves

A concept of right and wrong, good and evil, is reintroduced into our lives by the program. Some people ask in panic, "Do you really mean at this time in history, to reintroduce the devil—hooves, horns, and all?" Well, we really don't know what this time in history has to do with it. The hooves and horns are important only because we wear them ourselves.

So our answer is yes, the devil in us, the cause of our troubles, must be reintroduced and understood to be conquered. We are at the root of our own troubles; we are our own devils. And until we act to release ourselves of our selves, we will continue to slip and suffer.

Have I conquered myself?

> Higher Power, with your grace
> may I recognize my own devil
> and turn it over to you so that
> with your help it may be conquered.

Today I will restrain myself by

God help me to stay clean and sober today!

Having a Higher Power

Our program is spiritual. To work the program, we need to recognize a Higher Power. New knowledge becomes available through new instruments. We did not have much knowledge of the stars until the telescope or much knowledge of germs until the microscope. You can think of the Twelve Steps as an instrument—a means to realizing and remembering you have a Higher Power.

When we want to explore what lies beyond the five senses, we have to use an instrument that reaches beyond these senses. When we sincerely ask our Higher Power, it will show us an answer. Maybe not with writing on the wall, but we will be guided. After all, how did we get to this program?

Am I in touch with my Higher Power?

Higher Power, help me use the
Twelve Steps as an instrument to gain
knowledge of your presence in my life.

*Today I will improve my conscious contact
with my Higher Power by*

God help me to stay clean and sober today!

Being moved by ideals

Our new life is deeply moved by powerful ideals. Many of our pursuits fall apart and then we must regroup, perhaps many times, before our goals become sound again. But we must remember to keep our ideals in mind. We learn from our setbacks and know that they indicate we are reaching for and moving toward a perfect program and ideal spirituality. There is no one among us who is perfectly clean and sober.

Working a good program requires no accolades, only high ideals. The speakers at our meetings are not saints or prophets but nameless people. They tell their stories and deliver their messages informally, yet better than if the event had been staged. Together our unknown names and our new lives emerge from the ruins, and we form a body of our Higher Power's beautiful children.

Do my actions reflect the highest ideals?

> Higher Power, when my ideals
> try my faith, let me know that
> nothing is too good to be true.

The ideal I will strive toward today is

God help me to stay clean and sober today!

Becoming reasonable

Being ungrateful and feeling sorry for ourselves is a great self-destroyer. Often we feel that we know all the *reasons* to be grateful and to *not* feel sorry for ourselves, but we don't know how to be *reasonable* about our feelings. Being reasonable is not a strong virtue of addicts.

Quite often we find we have to pray for reasonableness, then simply cling to the program and the fellowship when feelings of ungratefulness overtake us.

Am I a more reasonable person than I was before?

> Higher Power, even though I know
> all the reasons, I am not always
> reasonable. Help me to
> become more reasonable.

Today I will try to be reasonable about

God help me to stay clean and sober today!

Removing the defects

Ralph Waldo Emerson once wrote, "No change of circumstances can repair a defect of character." For us, this is the absolute truth. If we are impossible to live with, getting another spouse will not change our disagreeableness. If we constantly bum from friends, changing friends will not make us less of a bum. If we are inconsiderate to our neighbors, moving to another state will not make us more considerate.

But working our character-defect Steps *can* remove our undesirable characteristics. In fact, working these Steps will help us *want* to give up our faults.

Am I rid of all my defects of character?

Higher Power, help me realize that the only way to change my character defects is to change my character defects.

The defects I will work on today are

God help me to stay clean and sober today!

Expressing good

Often we find ourselves thinking in terms of completing tasks rather than of expressing good. We view interruptions as frustrating delays, when they can be opportunities to glorify our Higher Power. Instead of saying, "How much can I accomplish today?" try restating your goal as, "How much good can I express today?" In expressing good, we accomplish much.

Our primary task each day is to express the nature of Infinite Spirit. We can consider a day to be fruitful if its spiritual demands have been perceived and fulfilled. Responding to setbacks with peace and love is much easier when we know that our main job in this life is to express good.

How much good have I expressed today?

Higher Power, help me to
remember throughout this day
that no task or plan is more important
than expressing your love.

Today I will express good by

God help me to stay clean and sober today!

OCTOBER 22

Tending spiritual needs

The less that is said about the physical nature of our disease, the more will be said of our spiritual needs. Our program is a set of suggestions for spiritual health that has worked to get many well. We have found that attending to our physical needs is not enough; we must tend to our spiritual needs as well.

When we're able to shut out the thoughts of the ego and close in on our spiritual feelings, we have a firm foundation for spiritual growth. As confident as we may be of our own thinking, we can hardly guide ourselves alone. Only adherence to spiritual principles and to a Higher Power can make a lasting difference in our lives.

How is my spiritual health?

Higher Power, help me
live my life closer to you.

Today I will enhance my spiritual health by

God help me to stay clean and sober today!

OCTOBER 23

Taking just a little

If we are trying to stay clean and sober while drinking a little beer or smoking a little pot, we are missing the mark. We can never know sobriety and cleanness under those conditions. Our programs cannot be effective or honest if we use any type of mind-altering chemical.

If you sincerely want the freedom, serenity, and joy of a drug-free existence, doing "a little" will never get it for you.

Have I learned that taking just a little invariably ends up in taking way too much?

Higher Power, show me the ways
I try to trick myself into using
mind-altering chemicals
and keep me from them.

Today I will remember my powerlessness by

God help me to stay clean and sober today!

Meditating

In our old lives we were busy giving orders, making demands, and directing others. Now we find it is time to try to listen. Prayer is talking to your Higher Power; meditation is listening to your Higher Power. There are as many types of meditation as there are individuals. We find that daily meditation is vital to keeping perspective.

Have I learned to meditate?

> I pray that I may learn
> to listen to my Higher Power
> so that I may be in harmony
> with the Higher Forces.

*Today I will listen to my
Higher Power by meditating about*

God help me to stay clean and sober today!

Remembering well

Do we remember how important preventive talk is for our fellowship and for our program? Drug-alogues and drunk-alogues are fine for getting to know each other in open meetings. But if we constantly sit around in social groups expounding on the "good times"—when we were abusing drugs and booze—what are we really doing?

Are we trying to tell ourselves drugs are really beneficial? Are we trying to fit in where we don't belong? Are we forgetting the pain and disaster? Are we ignoring the new beauty we have found? Preventive talk makes us aware of the tendency to expound on the "good old days." Preventive talk is necessary to keep our heads straight.

Do I remember the consequences well?

Higher Power, when I am tempted
to talk or think about the "good old days,"
let me remember the "bad old days."

Today I will look back at

God help me to stay clean and sober today!

Avoiding greed

Greed enslaves us to material things and diverts our values from the spiritual. As lust binds us to the animal plane, greed binds us to the material plane. We start to worship possessions. We begin to place love for the material before love for all living things or for our Higher Power. Greed can harden our conscience and become the greatest of slave drivers.

As we work to be free from drugs, we must work to be free from greed or we will always be slaves. Greed will make us into liars, hypocrites, robbers, bribers, and extortionists. Living like that, we cannot stay clean and sober for long.

Have I stopped being so materialistic?

**Higher Power, in your infinite mercy
show me that material greed
will only enslave me. Set me free.**

*Today I will give the following
material thing away*

God help me to stay clean and sober today!

Affecting those around us

Addiction is not a lone disease; it is sur-rounded by people who play a part in keep-ing the cycle going. These people—usually family, peers, co-workers, and sometimes even therapists—experience offshoots of the disease.

When a person gets stoned, those around him or her most likely react negatively. The addict reacts to their reaction by getting stoned again. So the downward cycle contin-ues. We need to be aware that the loved ones around us may be in need of help also. They become a part of our illness and need a way out just as much as we do.

Do I try to empathize with those close to me?

Higher Power, may I not expect my
abstinence to make the ones around me
"shape up," because they have been a
part of my illness for a long, long time.

*Today I will examine my impact
on those around me and*

God help me to stay clean and sober today!

Harmonizing conflicts

Our doubts and conflicts are strong reminders that we are not living harmoniously with our Higher Power's will for us. These conflicts grow out of our own attempt to give meaning and significance to our lives, rather than letting our Higher Power fill our lives with meaning and significance. Our own meaning is usually based on ego, money, and pleasure.

The meaning we desire comes through love, patience, and kindness, practices we often resist. If we lived according to our Higher Power's will, doubts and conflicts would not exist. We have gauges to measure our conscious contact. Harmony in our lives means we are working with our Higher Power. Conflict in our lives means we are straying from our Higher Power.

Is my life full of harmony?

> Higher Power, keep me on course;
> keep me from drifting away
> from your will for me today.

*I will peacefully work at resolving
the following conflict today by*

God help me to stay clean and sober today!

Thirteenth-Stepping

Thirteenth-Stepping is the act of moving too fast too soon, confusing lust for love. Some recovering addicts latch on to a newcomer in the fellowship, attempting to fulfill their own sexual desires. This has been called Thirteenth-Stepping.

Newcomers—who are feeling ashamed, helpless, and lonely—are only too glad to grab on to someone for a little security. But newcomers need, above all, to learn to stay clean and sober. To Thirteenth-Step a person only makes one concentrate on the relationship rather than on the program.

Do I know how to Twelfth-Step without getting too involved?

Higher Power,
help me to stop with the Twelfth Step.

Today I will look at my sexuality and

God help me to stay clean and sober today!

Following directions

At times we are so squirrelly nothing seems to make much sense. This is not an unusual predicament for people who abuse drugs. At times like these we're better off following the advice of other recovering addicts, whether it seems to make sense or not.

We have proved that our judgment is not what it could be. We have nothing to lose by following directions from those who love us and have experienced our behaviors. When confused, we must decide to take our bodies to meetings. Our heads will follow.

Am I receptive to the healthy suggestions of others?

Higher Power, may I learn to
turn to others for guidance
when I know my own head is shot!

Today I will seek help from

God help me to stay clean and sober today!

Exercising our power

We can use. Our Higher Power won't stop us. It won't take a joint out of our hand, tell the doctor not to give us tranquilizers or pain pills, or lock the door to the corner bar. But our Higher Power will give us the strength to refuse that first fix, pill, or drink. It is only necessary for us to practice that refusal.

No is an excellent word to use. Other fancy refusals will work, but *no* works best of all. After we have accepted the power to refuse mind-altering chemicals, we are given the power to work the steps. Our Higher Power gives us this power, but we have to exercise it ourselves.

Do I exercise my God-given power wisely?

Higher Power, help me to exercise
the power you have already given me.

*Today I will ask my Higher Power
for the power to*

God help me to stay clean and sober today!

NOVEMBER 1

Being inspired

Within any problem lies a seed of opportunity. Solutions to knotty circumstances come through spiritual inspiration. If we stay clean and sober, we can sense the inspiration. Instead of dragging us down, our problems can take us to new heights. Didn't our addiction bring us a spiritual awakening?

Our Higher Power's promises are sure. With every fear, we will hear that voice from within that stills our troubled minds.

Do I feel inspired?

I pray that I may do all I do with love and leave the results to my Higher Power.

I will seek inspiration today by

God help me to stay clean and sober today!

NOVEMBER 2

Becoming selfless

Only through the grace of our Higher Power can we feel peace and serenity. We know that self and self-based decisions end in pain. We have to replace self with love. If our hearts are full of our egos, there is no room for a Higher Power.

We begin to become selfless when we recognize that we need a Higher Power in our lives. We have learned from experience that no other way works for us. This does! The only point in talking about self is to know what we're trying to be free of, what we're substituting for a Higher Power.

Am I a selfless person now?

> Higher Power, let me put a
> little more of you into a place
> where I still have much self.

I will do things for others today, such as

God help me to stay clean and sober today!

Expressing gratitude

Gratitude is more than just being thankful. The *principle* of gratitude is a moral responsibility. If we are truly grateful, we will help others achieve what we have achieved. Next is the *priority* of gratitude. As soon as we know that God has changed our lives, we must let nothing interfere with what we know to be right.

The *propriety* of gratitude shows us that our Higher Power is not a respecter of persons, and we deserve its grace as much as anyone else does. Then the *purpose* of our gratitude is not entirely for the benefit of the one blessed. The purpose is to shed light on the *one* who blessed us.

Do my actions reflect my gratitude?

> Higher Power, help me always
> to remember to be grateful for
> what I have been blessed with
> and let me fully understand
> the magnitude of gratitude.

I will show my gratitude today by

God help me to stay clean and sober today!

NOVEMBER 4

Expressing love

Our fellowship is saturated with love and caring. We can touch one another and know that it comes from the Spirit. In the beginning, some confuse this love with sexual desire. A man may cringe when first embraced by another man, but the love we receive from our Higher Power is pure and needs no justification.

An embrace is an embrace of love. Now, we can freely express our love for each other. It's the same love that flows from our Higher Power. All true expression of love is good.

Do I know how to express my love outwardly?

Higher Power, let me express love
from you in some way today,
if only by touching another's hand.

Today I will openly express my love to

God help me to stay clean and sober today!

Giving joy

We deserve to have beautiful things and need not continue disparaging and punishing ourselves for our past behavior. If someone wants to give us something, we can accept it! They have a right to the joy of giving, and we have a right to the joy of receiving.

We also have a right to the joy of giving so others may receive. We can give material things, we can give moral support, we can give a friendly ear, and, best of all, we can give love. These are the beautiful things.

Have I learned to give?

Higher Power, help me to be able to give and to receive in a true and loving spirit.

Today I will give something of value to

God help me to stay clean and sober today!

NOVEMBER 6

Welcoming new ideas

No group has a harness on the program or on our Higher Power's will. Out of new assemblies emerge various thoughts on intervention and recovery. Provided that the program's main purpose is not forgotten, new and creative endeavors can enlighten us.

If we are narrow-minded, we miss opportunities to help others and to progress spiritually. Book-thumpers, hardnosers, do-it-on-your-own-timers—all of us contribute. And those who need our particular brand of help will be brought to us by our Higher Power.

Am I receptive to new and different ways?

Higher Power, as you help me to
keep an open heart,
help me to keep an open mind.

Today I will look for new ideas by

God help me to stay clean and sober today!

NOVEMBER 7

Pleasing ourselves

Many of our character defects stem from a motive to be acceptable on a social level. We worry about our popularity, our career prospects, our financial future, our reputation, and so on. By trying to please others, we exaggerate our real capabilities and may even lie to impress people.

We sometimes agree to do favors for others when we really can't or when we don't even want to. We become resentful. Others resent us or find us unreliable for not living up to our promises. We're not here to please people for the sake of pleasing people. We're here to please our Higher Power. Just knowing this causes many of our character defects to fade.

Do I know it's not necessary to please everybody all the time?

> Higher Power, show me how to please you and me and how to stop worrying about pleasing others.

I will try to please myself today by

God help me to stay clean and sober today!

Opportunities for growth

Any time spent growing spiritually is sacred. We're taking advantage of an opportunity to enhance the quality of our existence. When we were drinking or using, we may have felt a lot of quantity in our lives—a lot of parties, a lot of people, a lot of drugs. But the quality of our lives, of our relationships with people and with our Higher Power, was poor.

Every day finds many occasions for spiritual growth. We've already let many chances slip away. When we have a chance to grow, we need to take it. We can little afford to be hesitant or lazy, to waste our remaining opportunities for growth.

Do I recognize the opportunities all around me?

> Higher Power, show me what I can do
> today to make myself more worthy
> of the precious time given to me.

Today I will look for opportunities to grow by

God help me to stay clean and sober today!

Dropping our delusions

While using mind-altering chemicals, we often operated under delusions of grandeur. We thought we didn't have to take anything from anybody. We were confident we could handle everything. But if we remember correctly, when the landlady said, "Get out," we got out. When the police said, "Get in," we got in.

Actually, we were pushed around a lot. By letting go of false pride, we clear the way for real confidence.

Have I left my delusions behind?

> Higher Power, I am grateful
> for the freedom that comes with
> not having to be devious.

I will cultivate humility today by

God help me to stay clean and sober today!

Equal chances

So-called hopeless ones exist in almost every Twelve Step group. Included on this list are people who seem different from us. We feel that our chances of recovery are better than theirs. Sometimes our minds twist the facts so that we can feel superior.

Do we forget that we have *all* abused mind-altering chemicals? Do we forget that our common bond is a loving Higher Power, as we understand it—*not* our background, sexual orientation, age, or mental state? Our situations are many and varied. Anyone who has the desire to stay clean and sober and to start by being honest can make it.

Our Higher Power loves all of us, and we all have equal chances.

Do I extend my hand to all, even those I see as different from myself?

Higher Power, help me to see every person as being loved by his or her Higher Power.

Today I will work on my prejudices by

God help me to stay clean and sober today!

NOVEMBER 11

Trusting God's love

Trusting that our Higher Power wants the best for us also means trusting that it wants the best for our loved ones. God works through everyone. We can't believe that our Higher Power has led us through rebellion, pain, and suffering to this fellowship without believing it also guides everyone else.

Our Higher Power reaches people in different ways. We sometimes don't understand the wisdom behind all this. All we can do is carry the message by being an example; the rest is in our Higher Power's hands.

Do I feel secure knowing we are all guided by a Higher Power?

> Higher Power, I entrust all those
> who are dear to me to your
> never failing care and love.

*Today I will express my trust in my
Higher Power's love by*

God help me to stay clean and sober today!

Working the program

Who can adequately describe the serenity and fulfillment found in working the program through the years full of hard times and good times? Who can fully express the feelings of acceptance and peace we can now find when in the midst of chaos? How can we share the joy that spiritual growth has embedded into our lives?

For those who have lived in the depths of despair and suffering, passing into this new state of being is truly a miracle. And we know surely that this is available to all who are willing to work for it.

Am I willing to work the program wholeheartedly at all times?

> Higher Power, help me remember
> always that working my program
> is the only way for me.

*Today I will work the program
especially hard by*

God help me to stay clean and sober today!

Gaining peace of mind

Even though many of us were certainly ready to take the First Step—to admit that we were addicts—we balked at taking the following eleven Steps. We felt it would be ridiculous or too much work, or we denied the existence of a Higher Power.

When we started to hurt bad or began to reach for that first fix, pill, or drink, we woke up. We remembered and longed for the promise of peace of mind contained in those Steps. The PROMISE! Then we made a decision to work these Steps and to earn that promise.

Do I have peace of mind?

> Higher Power,
> the plan is up to you;
> the decision is up to me.

My plan for working all the Steps today is

God help me to stay clean and sober today!

Practicing principles

Reading, discussing, studying, thinking, or any other form of intellectual pursuit may play a role in helping us find our Higher Power. But we don't experience our Higher Power unless we put our principles into action. When we practice our principles, we set ourselves free so that our behavior does not stand between us and our Higher Power.

The insights we get from reading, discussing, studying, thinking, and so on are healthy food for thought. To gain the *freedom* that comes from *feeling* our Higher Power, we practice the principles.

Have I stopped intellectualizing about God?

> Higher Power, remind me that insight
> is not freedom and help me do
> what is necessary to find and to
> know you completely.

I will put my principles into action by

God help me to stay clean and sober today!

Seeking spirituality

Spiritual growth is an urge and a quest. The urge comes from within, and the quest, which is an outward manifestation, comes from the urge. Our quest suffers considerably when we make mind-altering chemicals our Higher Power. The urge for spiritual growth is still within us, but we have either lost sight of or have yet to find our true purpose. Staying chained to our addiction only keeps us from a meaningful destiny.

For us the quest is our program. While the urge for spiritual growth is always an individual one, we are privileged to share the same quest in our fellowship.

Have I joined the common quest?

**Higher Power, let my quest
for spiritual growth be in keeping
with my true purpose.**

*Today I will seek to fulfill my
urge for spiritual growth by*

God help me to stay clean and sober today!

NOVEMBER 16

Finding the real world

Our old ideas were often based on misconceptions of how the world was treating us. These misconceptions don't die easily, and it's hard to realize that the evils of the world were not what made us suffer. We made ourselves suffer. Our aimless rebellion only led us farther down the road of destruction.

There can be no denying that our lifestyle contributed greatly to all the evils. We are reminded of the character who said, "I have found the enemy establishment pig, and he is me!" We come to this realization, and we're suddenly aware of how beautiful the world is when we just let it be!

Have I found the real world?

> Higher Power, if the world reflects
> what I see in myself, let me see love,
> beauty, and kindness.

I will explore the real world today by

God help me to stay clean and sober today!

NOVEMBER 17

Finding happiness

How often we mistake pleasure for happiness! Many people enjoy every pleasure on earth, yet they are sad and lonely. Pleasure comes from the world, something outside us. As we learned from our drug-related experiences, pleasure can be deceiving and ungratifying. Pleasure left us no rewards but exacted a heavy toll. The more we sought unrealized dreams, the more unfulfilled we became.

Happiness comes from within, from being secure in knowing that we are loved and that our Higher Power loves us. We will know true happiness when we lose sight of ourselves through our love for our Higher Power.

Have I found happiness?

> Higher Power, show me that
> happiness comes from
> actively experiencing you in my life.

> *Today I will express my
> Higher Power's love by*

God help me to stay clean and sober today!

Striving for progress

We are not perfect. And because we are not perfect, we cannot expect to work the program perfectly. We don't benefit from sitting around feeling sorry for ourselves because we don't work the Steps to perfection. We only divert energy from working the Steps better.

All that's necessary is to make an honest effort at progress. Instead of feeling overwhelmed by all we have to do, we just have to be willing to do it. We are not perfect. We only *strive* for progress.

Am I still trying?

> Higher Power, let me be satisfied
> with my progress and not expect
> perfection from an imperfect being.

I will strive to progress spiritually today by

The chains that bind

Our self-centeredness and resentments are the chains that bind us. It makes little difference whether these faults are outstanding or subtle, whether they are justified or unjustified. We are still in a bind.

It matters little whether we are held by a slender thread or by a heavy rope. If we are anchored, we won't be freed until we decide to break the bond that holds us. A thin thread may be more easily broken, but we must decide to break it or it will stay put.

Unless our attachment to negative attitudes and actions is broken, our union with the Divine Source is hindered.

Have I broken free of my bonds?

Higher Power, help me discover
and release the character defects
that keep me from uniting with you.

*Today I will try to break free of
self-centeredness by*

God help me to stay clean and sober today!

NOVEMBER 20

Living in fellowship

Without our fellowship, many people would not be able to cross the line to sanity. Letters and visits keep us close to those who are far from meeting places. The fellowship is a joy and a necessity, and many of us believe it is a divine gift from our Higher Power.

Perhaps nothing else exists that can so completely multiply all our joys and divide all our grief.

Have I given what I can to the fellowship today?

Higher Power, may I do one deed
today that will increase the
beauty of our fellowship.

Today I will enjoy the fellowship by sharing

God help me to stay clean and sober today!

Practicing HOW

Principles, principles, principles. We talk so much about the principles of the Twelve Steps, but exactly what are they? HOW—honesty, open-mindedness, and willingness are surely key ones. By working the Twelve Steps, we live and breathe these three principles.

Do I practice honesty, open-mindedness, and willingness at all times?

Higher Power, help me be
honest, open-minded, and willing
every hour of this day.

*I will practice honesty, open-mindedness,
and willingness today by*

God help me to stay clean and sober today!

NOVEMBER 22

Counting our blessings

We have passed from death into life. We know that a powerful life force flows through us and a new and beautiful serenity is ours. What we once despised, we now cherish. We cease to find the world of drugs attractive.

This is a blessing and a miracle, for at one point we were among those considered to be the hopeless ones. Let's thank our Higher Power for our spiritual understanding and for the blessings of a clean and sober life.

Do I count my blessings each day?

Higher Power, I give thanks
from the depths of my heart and soul
for the blessing of my new life.

*Today I will look at my blessings,
one by one, and*

God help me to stay clean and sober today!

NOVEMBER 23

Being consistent

What we believe today is always subject to change tomorrow. We change and grow in many ways. We don't have to adhere to yesterday's words just because we said them in public. We may have received new data since then! We don't have to grapple with our memories so that we won't say something that contradicts past words. We live always in a new day.

We can trust ourselves and our Higher Power if our words and messages come from "the still small voice within." We must remember that what was necessary for us yesterday may not be what we need today.

Am I always open to growth, to change, to new views and ideas?

Higher Power, help me demonstrate
my consistent need to grow by
helping me be flexible.

Today I will question my beliefs about

God help me to stay clean and sober today!

Looking for substitutes

Therapy is no substitute for the program. Religious doctrine is no substitute for the program. Words are no substitute for the program. Intelligence is no substitute for the program. Heroic acts are no substitute for the program. "Easy does it" is no substitute for the program. Education is no substitute for the program.

Sex is no substitute for the program. A warm heart is no substitute for the program. A job is no substitute for the program. Only action—only the Steps—are going to get it for us. There are no substitutes.

Do I realize there's no quick and easy route?

Higher Power, may I stop playing games,
may I stop using excuses, and may
I do what I can in my program today.

I will work the program extra hard today by

God help me to stay clean and sober today!

Feeling alive

Not one of us has tasted the success of our sobriety and cleanness until we have awakened to a glorious day. It is made up of boundless energy, limitless joy, and knowing that whatever our Higher Power wills for us is good.

It tastes of spring to meet the day with the thrill of being alive. On these days we can feel a true spiritual joy that comes from feeling like a corpuscle in the body of our Higher Power.

Do I savor life?

Thank you, Higher Power,
for this day. Whatever your will is for me,
I know it is good.

I will enjoy being alive today by

God help me to stay clean and sober today!

Sharing opinions

At first, *really hearing* fellow addicts is an exciting experience. We may charge off explaining our insights at meetings and social gatherings. We truly need to share in this manner, but it should not affect us too much when other people don't accept our pearls of wisdom. What may be a gem for us could be a mere pebble for another.

So when others shoot us down for something we've said, we needn't take it too personally. What is right for one may not be right for another; however, we all have the right to express our opinions.

Do I share my views freely with others?

Higher Power, may my sharing not be imposing, and may I not take opinions as personal insults or rejections.

Today I will share my deepest insights with

God help me to stay clean and sober today!

NOVEMBER 27

Knowing our Author

It's important to know the Author of our hopes and desires. If we don't understand the force that guides us, and why we follow, anything can lead us anywhere. The Steps are helpful tools in getting to know our Author. They are a personal path to our Higher Power and give us more direction than we have ever experienced before.

Our lives are written in the *now*, the present. The past cannot be erased, so forget about it. The future cannot be determined before the present, so stop daydreaming. Live in the now, the present—live when your story happens so you experience it and learn and grow from it. Only today's activities are recorded today.

Who is the Author of my life?

May today be written by the
Supreme Author.

I will try to make today's page beautiful by

God help me to stay clean and sober today!

Being an individual

Because we work the same Steps everyone else in the program works and associate with other people in similar circumstances, we may sometimes question our individuality and the uniqueness of our personalities.

Personality is what we wish others to see in us. It's an impression and reflects our desire for recognition. It's important to remember that each of us is unique and has a talent waiting to be expressed. *Individuality* is the expression of our unique gift—it's what our soul longs for.

Our program teaches us to use our individuality. It's not necessary to worry about personality when we are meeting life's conditions as an individual driven by our Higher Power. Personality comes naturally, and is noticeably uncontrived, when we express our individuality.

Am I a true individual?

Higher Power, help me get past my personality so I may meet you face to face, as an individual bearing no false fronts.

Today I will express my individuality by

God help me to stay clean and sober today!

NOVEMBER 29

Finding friendship

We have friends we dance with or play sports with. This is friendship on a pleasure plane. Then we have friends in our professions and jobs. These friendships are on a different plane of common interests. Next is the identity and intellectual plane where we discuss favorite topics. But the highest and most beautiful plane of friendship is one in which we share the same spiritual quest.

We have the glory, through this fellowship, of experiencing immediate communion and intimacy with our people wherever we go. Such friendships last as long as the solution, which is our common bond.

Have I found a multitude of friends?

Higher Power, thank you for
blessing me with a world full of friends
who share my spiritual quest.

Today I will offer my friendship to

God help me to stay clean and sober today!

Lives worth saving

For many of us, the prospect of death was not a big thing. In fact, while we were using, many of us would have preferred to die. So it may not have seemed like much of a favor when our Higher Power saved our lives.

But our Higher Power also showed us that our lives were *worth* saving. This was the big step for us. We deserved to live! We were worth saving! We were not the wretches we had made ourselves out to be!

How glorious to have our Higher Power show us how we could do its work—how we could carry the message and be worth something to countless others!

Do I value my life highly?

> Thank you, Higher Power,
> for showing me that I am
> worth saving after all.

I will enhance my self-worth today by

God help me to stay clean and sober today!

DECEMBER 1

A rewarding way of life

Let us pause today and ask ourselves, *Why have I chosen this new way of life?* To the sick and weary, recovery seems a long, hard road to travel. We'd like an easier path, yet we know it wouldn't satisfy us. Using mind-altering chemicals—taking the easy path—ceased to satisfy us. We had no recourse but to join the fellowship.

We come to realize that the only path to cleanness and sobriety is to reach an understanding of and to become one with our Higher Power. Yes, the way is sometimes hard, but the rewards are many and great.

Do I relish my new way of life?

Higher Power, may I not falter
because the way is hard
but rejoice because the rewards are great.

Today I will enjoy my new way of life by

God help me to stay clean and sober today!

DECEMBER 2

The blessing of burdens

Those with the greatest burdens may be the most blessed, if they choose to take on the challenges before them. Somehow, the richness of joy is measured in direct proportion to the degree of suffering. Each of us has felt the joy of achievement. The intensity of what we've overcome influences the depth of that joy.

Before the blooms appear so hopefully in spring, the barren winter must come and go. To bring out the best in us, we have to overcome the obstacles of life. We ask our Higher Power for the strength to deal with and to accept them daily.

Have I grown as a result of my difficulties?

> Higher Power, help me accept my
> problems as blessings in disguise.

Today I will shoulder my heaviest burden and

God help me to stay clean and sober today!

DECEMBER 3

Finding the way

We are all meant to travel by the directions our Higher Power gives us. Many paths and modes of transportation lie before us. Many teachers are conveniently situated to help guide the way.

We need to remember that only our Higher Power can show us the whole way. If we open our hearts and minds to our Higher Power, it may work through us and our destined path will become obvious.

Am I on the way?

> Higher Power, may I begin to know
> the way, and as I go along,
> may more be revealed to me.

I will seek to find the way today by

God help me to stay clean and sober today!

DECEMBER 4

Being under a new influence

Under the influence of drugs, nothing was real. This is one of the hallmarks of an addict. A good day wasn't really much more satisfying than a terrible one because we always had the feeling of being on the periphery, of being on the outside looking in.

The good days provided no joy; they were unfulfilling. With a sickening awareness, we often played a sadistic game—we knew our actions were hurting ourselves as well as others. At the same time we felt very misunderstood, thinking, *Don't they know we don't want to be this way?*

Am I under a new influence now?

Higher Power, help me slow down today and have courage to live in the now.

I will fully experience today by

God help me to stay clean and sober today!

DECEMBER 5

Living a clean life

When we talk about being clean and sober, we're not talking about any kind of trance, ecstasy, or high. We're not talking about the aloof, alienated philosopher who withdraws from society nor the rigid, unbending fanatic who screams for temperance. The sobriety and cleanness we refer to is not an extreme. It's living well one day at a time.

We enjoy our children and friends, live life to the fullest, and are engaged in many activities. Some of us are great lovers, husbands, wives, or leaders. We all, at times, suffer anguish and doubt. No, we are not drawn away from life but to it.

Am I living today well?

> Higher Power, let your irresistible
> burning love shine through me.

Today my plan for living well is

God help me to stay clean and sober today!

Accepting joy

In our drug-free lives, we frequently experience great joy and happiness. But sometimes, because of our past, we feel so guilty that we don't accept this happiness. To avoid being happy, we'll even go so far as to create new problems.

The familiarity of being troubled is somehow comforting. Acknowledging and releasing this false need clears the way for the journey along the spiritual path. Accepting our Higher Power's gifts of joy enables us to spread joy and to receive it in turn—to heighten our spirituality.

Have I learned how to accept joy and happiness?

> Higher Power, may I know in my heart
> that you love me and that I am
> worthy of being happy.

> *I will accept the joy
> that comes my way today by*

God help me to stay clean and sober today!

DECEMBER 7

Accepting responsibility

Our troubles are of our own making. At first it's hard to comprehend that our trials and tribulations are the result of choices *we've* made. Sometimes we ask ourselves, *Why does my Higher Power let these things happen to me?* This may be our Higher Power's way of saying, "You're on the wrong path! This is the way—take *this* path!" From suffering comes growth. Maybe we have to suffer before we've "grown" enough to realize our path.

The longer we fail to accept responsibility for our actions, the longer it takes to have a fulfilling relationship with our Creator. We have to acknowledge that our failures and hardships are ours and our doing. Society, our parents, or our Higher Power are not to blame.

Do I accept responsibility for all my actions?

Higher Power, may I turn to you
for guidance and stop blaming others
for my misfortunes.

*Today I will look at my personal responsibility
in relation to problems such as*

God help me to stay clean and sober today!

Going forward

Our lives have not come to a standstill. In fact, our lives began when we decided to stop using drugs. This program isn't a punishment but a glorious gift from our Higher Power.

Because we are recovering, we are stronger. If we feel we're at a standstill, we can move forward. When things are bad, we can change them to good. When things are good, we can improve them. With our Higher Power's guidance, we keep progressing and don't get stuck in a rut.

Am I out of all the old ruts?

Higher Power, may I realize
that this program is not a punishment
but a step forward with you.

Today I will take a step forward by improving

God help me to stay clean and sober today!

DECEMBER 9

Being healthy

Because we are clean and sober, we now confront matters we had previously overlooked or snubbed. One concern new to many of us is the importance of taking care of our bodies.

After years of mistreating ourselves, we can't expect to be perfectly healthy. Some conditions may be permanent. The next time we start to feel sorry for ourselves because our bodies are not perfect, let us breathe in and out and listen to our heartbeat. Can we say our Higher Power hasn't been good to us?

How is my spiritual health?

> Higher Power, help me to remember
> that mind and body are connected
> and to know that the healthier
> my thoughts are, the healthier
> my body will be.

I will improve my health today by

God help me to stay clean and sober today!

DECEMBER 10

Being loving people

Many of us considered ourselves to be loving people. When we learned that we weren't as loving as we'd made ourselves out to be, we became reproachful. We knew we couldn't truly love other people and presumed it was our fault. But our only fault was in not realizing that to give love we need to receive it. To give love, we need first to be open to receiving it from our Higher Power.

We didn't know that to find love we only needed to ask for it. When we feel love for our enemies, we know beyond a shadow of a doubt that our Higher Power is with us. We know in such situations that we could not produce this kind of love by ourselves.

Do I have the gift of love?

Higher Power, help me be willing to love any person you set in my path.

Today I will ask my Higher Power for love in my relationship with

God help me to stay clean and sober today!

DECEMBER 11

On the move

Do we remember the "geographical cure," when we rationalized that if we changed our location our problems would melt away? Some of us left a city. Some left a state. Others thought the communes had the answer. Some even sought the answer in other countries.

Wherever we went we always brought our selves along. Unless we changed our selves, no place in the universe could resolve our problems for us. Invariably, we found that our program was the only answer for us.

Have I changed within?

Higher Power, let me hear the
"still small voice within"
and know that change begins with me.

Today I will analyze my changes, including

God help me to stay clean and sober today!

DECEMBER 12

Dealing with turmoil

Our emotional reactions to people and events—not the people and events themselves—are the source of our turmoil and strife. Other people don't make our lives unbearable. The turmoil is not in the event but in our reaction to it.

If a friend slips and falls, do we react with, "Look what you've done to me"? Most likely, we'll offer a helping hand and some compassion. We don't take the happening personally. When we're upset or frustrated with others, we can choose to fill our hearts with anger, sadness, pain or—in the spirit of our Higher Power—with love and understanding.

Have I stopped reacting?

Higher Power, I pray that I may
gain strength in your love and turn away
the strife caused by fear and
uncontrolled emotions.

Today I will handle any frustration placidly by

God help me to stay clean and sober today!

DECEMBER 13

Restoring our sanity

We believe that our Higher Power can restore us to sanity. If we work on getting spiritually fit, we know our mental and physical problems will straighten out.

Our Higher Power can and will heal us. Our Higher Power can and will guide us. We believe in our Higher Power.

Am I sane?

Higher Power, teach me to believe that you can and will keep me sane.

I will work on staying sane today when confronting problems such as

God help me to stay clean and sober today!

DECEMBER 14

Giving it away

We can't give away what we don't possess. We can't teach others to live what we don't live. Before we tell others about the joys of a chemical-free existence, we must live that chemical-free existence. We must be spiritual.

Our Higher Power guides us to the people we need to carry the message to.

Do I give it away every day?

Higher Power, I pray that I may be a channel of your blessing to others.

Today I will give it away to

God help me to stay clean and sober today!

DECEMBER 15

Gaining understanding

Most of us have things happen in our lives that we don't understand. Many things we'll probably never understand and may not need to understand.

We have the most to gain by trying to understand recurring negativity. We can get insight from the fellowship, from the Steps, and from our sponsors. The cycle can be broken if we unmask old ideas and habits that initiate the recurrent misfortunes. When we understand the problem, we overcome it by seeking the seed of opportunity within.

How well do I understand myself?

Higher Power, help me to give up ideas
and habits that lead me down my
old path time and time again.

*Today I will look at the problems
and negativity in my life
and seek to understand them by*

God help me to stay clean and sober today!

Honesty

We have to learn to be rigorously honest with ourselves. If we can't be honest with ourselves, we can't be honest with others, we can't be honest with our Higher Power, and we can't expect to change.

If we call a cab to one address, and we are, in fact, at another, we can't expect the driver to find us much less pick us up. So it is with our Higher Power. If we ask to be healed of something but mistake our malady for another, we can't expect the change we'd hoped for.

We have to begin listening to how we really feel. Most of us have very tricky heads but very honest guts!

Do I acknowledge my gut-level honesty?

Higher Power, help me to know
where I'm really at and to accept it.

*Today I will explore my
gut reactions to things by*

God help me to stay clean and sober today!

DECEMBER 17

Remembering

We are survivors! We lived long enough to let our Higher Power save our lives. We managed not to OD or die of cirrhosis, in a car accident, in jail, or by a bullet. We somehow avoided meeting these and countless other horrible ends associated with our disease.

By the grace of our Higher Power, we may never have to live in that world again. If we forget where we came from, let us visit the detox units of our local hospitals. We will be reminded by observing addicts with DTs, brain damage, and many other injuries resulting from the abuse of mind-altering chemicals.

Do I remember where I came from?

Higher Power, let me never forget
where I came from and where I will
return to if I fail to live by your principles.

Today I will recall the past by

God help me to stay clean and sober today!

DECEMBER 18

Heeding the slogans

Our fellowship adheres to many slogans that might at first appear trite: Easy Does It, First Things First, Live and Let Live, One Day at a Time, Keep It Simple.

Many wise individuals developed these slogans from their experiences, and the phrases are anything but trite. The next time we hear them, let's consider if they're working in our lives. It may be the difference between working a good program or just staying off the stuff.

Do I fully understand and appreciate the meanings of our slogans?

Higher Power, let me learn
from the experiences of others.

The slogan I will create for today is

God help me to stay clean and sober today!

Expressing soul

Knowledge and understanding alone do not lead us to the new life. If that were the case, psychiatrists and psychologists would have better success rates with us. So what is the source of our success in finding our paths? It's our ability to follow our Higher Power's cues. It's being tuned in enough to feel and to act on the opportunities our Higher Power presents to us each day.

What comes from the soul originates from the Higher Power. Let us follow the prompting of our soul, so we may better learn what it means to live in the glory of our Higher Power. Acknowledging our Higher Power and applying what we learn from it is what makes us successful.

How well do I express my soul?

Higher Power, through the power
you have given me, may I make known
your beauty and love to others.

Today I will follow my Higher Power by

God help me to stay clean and sober today!

DECEMBER 20

Living abundantly

Leaving our drug-filled lives and turning to our Creator in this fellowship does not mean becoming mindless, spiritless, sexless robots. It doesn't mean all fun will be taken from us.

Being one with our Higher Power doesn't take life away. It gives us the opportunity to live a life of abundance. We learn to think, feel, and breathe with more perception and depth than we could have ever before imagined.

Is my life full and rich?

Higher Power,
let my eyes see the beauty,
let my ears hear the laughter,
let my body feel the joy,
and let my words spread the hope.

Today I will enrich my life by

God help me to stay clean and sober today!

DECEMBER 21

Knowing God loves us

No matter how bad we abused drugs, no matter how desperate we became, our Higher Power still gave us the opportunity to recover. We need never think that opportunity has passed us by. Our Higher Power's grace is limitless.

We must never feel that it's too late or that we have failed too often to be able to turn to our Higher Power. It loves us, and it is loving us *now, today, always*. All things are possible with our Higher Power, and it will always give us life and love unless we choose otherwise.

Can I feel my Higher Power's love now?

May I know that any day is an
acceptable day to seek love
and forgiveness from my Higher Power.

I will choose my Higher Power's love today by

God help me to stay clean and sober today!

DECEMBER 22

Inner guidance

The way is simple. It is through our Higher Power. Those who seek fulfillment through drugs, friends, or mysterious cults will be troubled and confused, for our Higher Power is within us. Only we can know what it has to say to us—not others.

Do I follow my conscience in all things?

Higher Power, today I will know and listen to the "still small voice within."

Today I will seek inner guidance by

God help me to stay clean and sober today!

DECEMBER 23
Choosing wisely

We choose our activities. What we focus on manifests in our lives. If we opt to go to drinking or to pot parties or to socialize with practicing addicts, we are setting ourselves up for failure by re-creating our old environment.

If we choose to associate with people who are clean and sober and spiritually driven, then we are more likely to grow to be clean and sober and spiritual. Our Higher Power will show us the way by disclosing these activities to us.

Do I always choose wisely?

Higher Power, may I learn to choose the activities that lead to growth, not despair.

Today I will choose the good by

God help me to stay clean and sober today!

DECEMBER 24

Accepting help

We sometimes find it difficult to accept anything from other people. We don't want to be obligated to them for love, money, or support. We don't want to feel we owe them something in return. We need to remember that all help comes from our Higher Power and that our Higher Power sometimes reaches us through other people. Knowing this empowers us to accept help graciously.

As long as we remain true to our spirituality, all things are right. It's only when we deviate from our true purpose that we make mistakes in accepting things. God loves us and will provide all things if we remain true to God's purpose.

Have I learned to accept help from others?

> Higher Power, I want to accept all gifts
> sent to me through you, be they
> mental, emotional, or material.

> *Today I will help*

God help me to stay clean and sober today!

DECEMBER 25

Accepting gifts

Giving is part of the holiday spirit. We need not lament because we don't understand the nature of giving. Many of us suffer on this day for reasons a little more subtle than usual. Though we don't realize it, many of us feel inadequate to the holiday spirit, which is so incredibly magnificent. We need to allow ourselves to dwell in this magnificence.

We are all children of our Higher Power. We can joyfully accept its gifts of love, peace, fellowship, sobriety, and cleanness. We will learn how to give in turn.

Do I feel the spirit of the holidays?

Thank you, Higher Power,
for your gifts to me today and every day.

Today I will share in the holiday spirit by

God help me to stay clean and sober today!

DECEMBER 26

Working today

As we approach a new year, many of us feel fear. We look back on the past and worry about the future. But if we remember we only have today, we can work to make that future better. We have found true friends in our fellowship, and this is a time to be with them.

Am I ensuring a fruitful future by working with all I've got today?

Higher Power, I pray for guidance
for today and for freedom from
worry about tomorrow.

Today I will work for the fellowship by

God help me to stay clean and sober today!

DECEMBER 27

Following our guide

The biggest danger for us is delusion. A delusion, once started, is unable to check itself. When we're no longer honest with ourselves, we lose sight of what is good for us.

But our knowing Guide will help us when we wander. If we're caught up in the midst of our delusion, at first we may ignore our Higher Power's lead. But a sincere request will always bring our Guide to our aid.

Do I follow my true Guide?

May I find the wisdom to call upon my Guide whenever I get caught up in my delusions.

Today I will check myself for delusions by

God help me to stay clean and sober today!

DECEMBER 28

Changing attitudes

Slowly we have to change destructive attitudes and bury our hate, resentment, anxiety, and jealousy. These can be replaced with love, patience, mercy, kindness, and gentleness.

When we practice these new attitudes, we break down old barriers. Our outlook on life will cease to consist of finding fault because someone forgot something, someone's judgment was bad, or someone acted selfishly. We learn to overlook these circumstances as our Higher Power does.

Have I changed my attitudes?

Higher Power, may my heart's desire be to change my attitudes and to see and reflect the glory of God in all living things.

Today I will appraise my current attitudes by

God help me to stay clean and sober today!

DECEMBER 29

Having faith

We find in our daily lives that there are people who don't realize a Higher Power. Some of these people may ridicule us for our beliefs, but we *need* faith to get better.

We rely on our Higher Power to help keep us from drugs and alcohol. We must remember to practice our principles and to maintain our beliefs so we will not be swayed by contrary opinions.

Am I a true believer?

Higher Power, I pray that I may have
the patience to love all people
no matter what their beliefs.

Today I will express my faith by

God help me to stay clean and sober today!

DECEMBER 30

Being friends

When we were using drugs we had many friends, many party friends. They were our friends until the bad times came. Where were they then? With our new understanding, friends take on a new meaning. Friendships become spiritual in nature. Are we ready to have friends?

Like begets like. If we are friendly, we will have friends. We needn't impose ourselves on friends but rather create hope and help in their lives. A kind word here, a brotherly act there—not great deeds, just accessibility. This is how we make ourselves worthy of being called friend.

Am I a true friend?

Higher Power, may I be able to offer hope
and help and acts of kindness
to the ones I call friends.

Today I will befriend

God help me to stay clean and sober today!

DECEMBER 31

Being less than perfect

It was not a perfect year. But is there ever a perfect year? Being clean and sober does not purport to offer perfection. It gives us a chance to strive for progress. When we keep our Higher Power in our thoughts and actions, we come closer to perfection all the time.

Despite the disappointments of our complex lives, we are finally beginning to learn how to live. We are finally making progress.

Am I content to be less than perfect?

Higher Power, I pray that I may continue
to strive for progress and be satisfied
to be an imperfect human.

I will enjoy my humanity today by

God help me to stay clean and sober today!

Index